THE MAKING
OF AN
INSURGENT

THE MAKING
OF AN
INSURGENT

An Autobiography: 1882-1919

by

Fiorello H. La Guardia

INTRODUCTION BY
M. R. WERNER

GREENWOOD PRESS, PUBLISHERS
WESTPORT, CONNECTICUT

Library of Congress Cataloging-in-Publication Data

La Guardia, Fiorello H. (Fiorello Henry), 1882-1947.
  The making of an insurgent.

  Reprint. Originally published: Philadelphia :
Lippincott, c1948.
  Includes index.
  1. La Guardia, Fiorello H. (Fiorello Henry), 1882-
1947. 2. Legislators--United States--Biography.
3. United States. Congress. House--Biography.
4. Mayors--New York (N.Y.)--Politics and government--
1898-1951. I. Title.
E748.L23A3 1985   974.7'1041'0924 [B]   85-24782
ISBN 0-313-22769-1 (lib. bdg. : alk. paper)

974.71
L181L

Reprinted with the permission of Lippincott and Crowell Publishers

Reprinted in 1985 by Greenwood Press
A division of Congressional Information Service, Inc.
88 Post Road West, Westport, Connecticut 06881

Printed in the United States of America

10 9 8 7 6 5 4 3 2 1

INTRODUCTION

WHEN ONE THINKS of Fiorello La Guardia—and a great many people in this and other nations will be thinking of him and missing him for many years—one thinks of a man of courageous integrity, impetuous righteousness, energetic ability and colorful passion. Those who disliked him—and, being a man of little caution, he made his enemies—will perhaps recall his choleric quality and his inflexible convictions. He was sure he was right, and he was not always sure other men were right.

There were people of all political parties and economic beliefs whom he respected greatly and worked with closely, and they were usually the kind of men and women who have meant most to the progress of American society. He told me once that he never claimed to be an intimate of Franklin D. Roosevelt's but that he had had the privilege of working with him intimately on important things. The late Senators George W. Norris and Robert M. La Follette were men La Guardia listened to and worked with. There were people whom he heartily despised and made a lot of trouble for.

I believe that next to Franklin D. Roosevelt Fiorello La Guardia was the most creative statesman whose services the American public has enjoyed in recent times. Because of the constructive and colorful twelve years he put in as Mayor of New York, people have forgotten to some extent the extraordinary service he performed during the fourteen years he served in the House of Representatives, and very few realize that his public service began even before then, when he worked as an American consular agent in Europe before the first world war, aided immigrants pouring into Ellis Island previous to that war, and fought for the civil liberties of striking garment workers before the Amalgamated Clothing Workers Union was organized. As the following autobiographical chapters reveal, La Guardia began to be concerned about the state of the world, and particularly that of his native United States, as soon as he was able to read the newspapers with any degree of concentration.

In the course of his Congressional career, La Guardia was on the progressive side of every domestic and foreign controversy in the years between the two world wars. During the first war he fought personally as an aviator, and during the second he worked feverishly as Director of Civilian Defense, as Mayor of the largest port of embarkation for troops and supplies in the country, and as American chairman of the Joint Canadian-American Defense Board. After the war, and after his retirement as New York's most effective Mayor, he became the most dynamic director of the United Nations Relief and Rehabilitation Administration.

La Guardia fought aggressively, shrewdly and amusingly for the things he believed in so intensely. He fought bitterly and sometimes hilariously against the evils he opposed. The achievements of this physically diminutive man who had so much irascible energy are so many that it seemed almost as if the United States had lost in his death a great social power plant.

Early in life La Guardia developed his principles and ambitions, which went hand in hand throughout his great career. He was eager to be a Congressman, and he loved being one, as he reveals in the following pages. It is obvious from the papers in his files that he also wanted to be Mayor of New York, where he was born and which he loved. He started running for Congress in 1914 and actually made it in 1916. He started running for Mayor in 1921 and actually made it in 1933. If he had lived longer, he would have liked to have gone back to Congress, either as a Senator or a Representative from New York.

The part of his autobiography which La Guardia was able to complete before his death on September 20, 1947, and which is herewith presented, covers his early activities in Arizona and New York, the development of his career abroad, his work with the Immigration Service, his practice as a young lawyer and Deputy Attorney General of the State of New York, early political campaigns, his first years in Congress, his war service in Italy during World War I, and his principal interests as a Congressman grappling with the post-war problems of World War I. In a later book about him, I shall attempt a full account of the remainder of his controversial and constructive career as Congressman, Mayor, Director-General of UNRRA, and columnist and radio commentator.

This book consists of the material Fiorello La Guardia dictated and edited during the last six months of his life, when I was working with him on the research for his autobiography. It comprises a complete account of his life, as he saw it, from 1882, when he was born, until 1919, when he returned to Congress from war service. In his case, unlike that of some other public figures, his early career was not one of mere play, growth and study. He could not afford much leisure, though he seemed to have plenty of fun, and he was too restless to wait for opportunities. He grasped tasks that other young men would have hesitated to undertake, and he learned whatever he needed to know as he went along. His early experiences foreshadow his later activities, and the personality he was born with was essentially the same as he later became famous for. My task in this book primarily has been permitting that personality to express itself through the material La Guardia left and organizing that material into chapters of autobiography. The task of telling the story of his entire career, appraising the manifold activities he engaged in and portraying the personality of the man as Congressman, Mayor and statesman-at-large remains to be done.

La Guardia's personality has been the subject of countless anecdotes and reminiscences since his untimely death. He had become more than a Congressman from New York and a mayor of that city. He became, in fact, a legendary hero to some people, who wrote him their troubles and ideas rather than sending them to their own Congressmen or mayors. He also became the object of vituperation by people who thought him a wild radical. The engraved stationery of brokers and bankers and the deckle-edged paper of retired men and women living on income from investments, among the huge number of letters in his files, contained the sharp criticism and the angry abuse, by and large. The ruled paper of the poor, worried about where their next batch of canned goods was coming from, usually contained the encouragement: "Go to it." He answered an incredible amount of this mail and read practically all of it.

Though formally a Republican—because he couldn't stomach Tammany in New York—La Guardia never hesitated to leave his party reservation whenever his views were different from those who controlled that party—and they were often different. Though he refused to be regular, La Guardia was as astute as the regulars at the game of politics, which, as this book shows, he early cultivated as his art. He knew well how to play politics, but he was never a political boss, or even a political leader. He built excellent machinery for getting elected each time he ran for Congress or for Mayor, but that machinery was stored without oil until the next election, when the rust was rubbed off, and the process started all over again. Thousands of enthusiastic citizens always offered their services to help run the La Guardia election machinery.

La Guardia's main tenet was that an officeholder, big or small, must give a "non-political, non-partisan administration." This was the basis of his faith in his ability to give good government. He felt that the reason William Jay Gaynor and John Purroy Mitchel, two of his predecessors as Mayor of New York, whom he admired greatly, had not completely succeeded was that they gave politicians something or recognized obligations to politicians. He was fiercely determined not to make the same mistakes.

In his close attention to details as Congressman, Mayor or radio commentator, La Guardia amazed friends and foes. He worked long hours at his desk, continued to work while riding in his car, chased around checking up on federal officials when he was in Congress, on city employees when he was Mayor. He helped plan and construct national defense, city improvements and developments, read most of the complaints of the citizens, and was frequently critical of his own associates and the press when he felt they did not appreciate what he was trying to do or were not helping him to do it.

His attention to minute detail sometimes made me think of a small shopkeeper with a big heart, who emerges from the back of the store whenever he hears the tinkle of the bell attached to the door, and seems to be saying, sometimes gruffly, but always sincerely: "I'm here; what do you want?" And yet, from watching La Guardia at work even during the last months of his life when he was in ill health, I got the impression of the most effective executive I had ever seen in action. He was deadly in his earnestness, brusque in his demands and never satisfied with his own results. Whenever he wrote an article, he was sure it wasn't good enough, and he fussed with it until the last possible moment before publication in the effort to make it better. At the same time, he had to an extraordinary degree the ability to make up his mind quickly and the instinct for the side of a controversy he was going to regard as right.

La Guardia's impatience and irascibility, of which much has been made, were part of his earnestness, for in spite of a gay comedian's sense of theatre, he was not a sanguine man. He was always too worried about the world to take it easily, and during those last terrible months when he was visibly wasting away, he tried to accomplish more than most men undertake in their prime. It was during that period that he dictated the last parts of this book, sandwiched in between letters to President Truman and Secretary of State Marshall, advice to people worried about increases in their rents or about losing their money to loan sharks. He kept up his constant warfare against boss rule in New York and used some of his remaining strength to try to persuade his own government not to tie political strings to relief of other nations and to be generous in its admission of displaced persons. And until the day of his death he remained the champion of displaced persons at home.

What made La Guardia such a good public speaker was that he was deeply sincere about whatever he was discussing and a great actor in his ability to make that sincerity felt. He studied carefully, but he talked extemporaneously. He told me that he had seldom written out a speech in advance when he talked on the floor of the House, merely taking with him sheaves of notes, statistics and reports he might need. I had lunch with him the day of the evening of his last public appearance, in Carnegie Hall to receive the One World Award. "How long are you going to talk, Major?" I asked. "As long as I can hold them," he said quickly. He wrote out his broadcasts and rehearsed them, but he was as likely as not to change them in mid-air. He liked fun, and realized perfectly when he was putting over a good joke in public. His speeches and radio talks, whether as Congressman, Mayor or commentator managed to be intimate and at the same time significant.

For all the publicity and acclaim which La Guardia received and courted, he was a singularly modest man. I remember his picking up a telephone one day in the spring of 1947 and saying to a man from whom he was seeking information for a radio broadcast: "Dr. Brown, my name's La Guardia. I don't know whether you remember me, but

I met you a few years ago," and then going on to ask for what he wanted.

All right, he changed the name of Sixth Avenue to the Avenue of the Americas, and he asked children to peach on their fathers when they were betting on the horses; he lost his temper violently and seemed to some men ungrateful for the work they had done with or for him. But millions of people will always love him for his statement: "When I make a mistake, it's a beaut," and many more millions will realize more and more as the record of his great career unfolds, that he was creatively on their side in every important public issue, internationally, nationally and locally, for about forty years.

M. R. WERNER

CONTENTS

THE MAKING
OF AN
INSURGENT

CHAPTER I

Arizona Influences

1

I SUPPOSE EVERY conventional autobiography should start with one's birth, hard times during childhood and a great deal of family background. There is no pretense that this is a conventional autobiography. It is my purpose to write an account of public service and personal experience, with emphasis on the many important issues involved and the men, women and children with whom I came into contact in various parts of the world.

I have a birth certificate to prove my birth in New York City on December 11, 1882. That should take care of that. That is more than my brother Richard had, for he was born later at Fort Sully, an Army post in the then Territory of Dakota, but never had legal proof that he was alive.

My parents were immigrants. Mother was born in Trieste, and Father was born in Foggia, Italy. I came along some three or four years after their passage through Castle Garden. Father was a musician. From what I learned later, the family had a modest but comfortable apartment in New York when I was born. Mother was a pretty little immigrant girl and had made friends in the neighborhood.

Two of these friends my mother had made, by the time I came along, were the mothers of sons who became associated with my activities in New York City. Mrs. Charles Kohler's son Charlie became a Tammany leader and a great influence in that organization. We always remained good friends, though I did put Charlie out of business. My mother's other friend was the mother of Dr. John Wade, who became during my administration Superintendent of Schools in New York, the greatest school system in the entire world. I had nothing to do with his promotion, but we developed a sentimental feeling for each other, though I did not meet him until I became President of the Board of Aldermen in 1920.

Mrs. Kohler was a sweet lady of Swiss origin. She was most kind to me at a time when I needed it. When I was a clerk in the Society for the Prevention of Cruelty to Children at $10 a week in 1906, Mrs. Kohler managed to feed and board me within my modest income during the three months that I held that job. She also took up the cudgels in my behalf politically or otherwise. When I was running for Congress in 1916 from a district in Greenwich Village, Charlie Kohler was a Tammany big shot in that Congressional district. One Saturday night when nearly every corner was covered with a truck and red lights and a campaign meeting, Mother Kohler was coming home from her Saturday night shopping, loaded with bundles, bags and baskets. She stopped at one of the street corner meetings to listen and heard a Tammany orator lambaste me, telling the people that I was an immigrant just arrived, nothing but a "wop," and not fit to represent the great 14th Congressional District in Washington. My opponent, then representing that great district in Congress, was President of the National Liquor Dealers' Association. Mother Kohler shouted out: "That's not so, that's a lie! Fiorello was born right in this district! And you wait till Charlie gets home, I'll fix him. Cut that out and tell the truth!" And did Charlie get it when he came home!

I was only a few months old when my father joined the Army. He was the leader of the 11th U.S. Infantry Band. We went through South Dakota, but of course I have very little recollection of our time there, just one hazy childhood memory of a prairie fire. From there the regiment was moved to Madison Barracks, Sacketts Harbor, New York, and then to Arizona.

All my boyhood memories are of those Arizona days. To me that is truly God's country—I love everything about it. Perhaps my memories of Arizona are so pleasant because I had a happy, wholesome boyhood. My parents were of the doting kind—too much love for their children and not the best of judgment in guiding their education; something for which I paid dearly in later years when I had to make up the deficiencies.

Our first Army station in Arizona was at Fort Huachuca, where we arrived in the late 'eighties. Its location, miles and miles from urban civilization, its barren hills and bleak surroundings made it exceedingly unpleasant and undesirable for grown-ups but a paradise for a little boy. We could ride burros. Our playground was not measured in acres, or city blocks, but in miles and miles. We could do just about everything a little boy dreams of. We talked with miners and Indians. We associated with soldiers, and we learned to shoot even when we were so small the gun had to be held for us by an elder. My family had a two-room 'dobe house, with a detached kitchen. The kitchen had a canvas roof, and the house had plank sides and flooring. It sure looked great to a small boy.

Our Army post school had one teacher, a soldier of British birth. I was too young to know how good he was as a teacher, but I did know that he wielded a mean ruler and certainly knew how to apply it to the calves of our legs, leaving black and blue marks as a reminder until the next application.

From Fort Huachuca our regiment was moved to Whipple Barracks, near Prescott, Arizona. My memories of Prescott are that it was the greatest, the most comfortable and the most wonderful city in the whole world, whatever anybody might say about New York or Paris. People were so nice. Father was popular in the town, and, as children of the Army bandmaster, my sister and I, though little kids, performed for all sorts of benefits. I played the cornet, and Gemma the violin, while Father accompanied us on the piano.

The setting of Prescott was about as beautiful as any I have ever seen since. I have indelible memories of the early morning grandeur of Point of Rocks, Granite Dell, San Francisco Peak and Thumb Butte.

Army life was quite different in the eighteen eighties and 'nineties from what it is today. The pay of an enlisted man was $9 a month. The food was real, honest-to-goodness he-man Army food. Soldiers were tough. They had to be to survive existing conditions. All the officers were West Point men. A first lieutenant was 'way past middle age before he was in line for promotion to a captaincy. The distinction between commissioned officers and enlisted men was great. And that distinction went all the way down to the kids on the post. It never bothered me very much because I did not adhere to such rules. I would just as soon fight with an officer's kid as I would with anyone else. Many of my experiences as an Army brat were useful to me when as a legislator I had to study bills affecting our Army and could apply this first-hand knowledge.

I attended the public school in Prescott. I thought it was a grand school. At first we had three or four teachers and later on a staff of five or six. They came from various parts of the United States. From what I heard later, I was a headache to every one of them. I have had a great deal to do with teachers since then: twelve years as Mayor, with 36,000 of them in our school system. Maybe it is sentiment, but that bunch of Arizona public school teachers still seems to me about the best in the whole world. And that does not mean that I was not walloped by them.

Lena Coover was my favorite, and I was taunted by the kids for being teacher's pet. She was the prettiest little thing. She looked so young. She came from Iowa Normal, and, as the Prescott job was her first, she was jittery about it. We were quick to catch her nervousness. We made the most of it. She learned a lot from us, and I used to tell her in later years that we, and not the Iowa Normal School, made her a teacher. On the first day she corrected my arithmetic paper. Some of the examples were wrong, and she did not notice them. The next day I purposely gave some wrong answers. Again the paper came back marked correct. Like the fresh kid I was, I went up to her desk the next day and said, "Look here, teacher, you better learn arithmetic if you are going to teach us," and I pointed out the mistakes to her. Was her pretty little face red! Well, she did learn arithmetic, and by the time we were through with her she could put us through the mathematical ropes. Miss Lena lives in Los Angeles, and I have seen her from time to time. The same mutual affection that existed during the time when I was the bane of her existence exists today. She thinks I am a great statesman, and I think she is a great teacher, which just about makes us even.*

2

What I saw and heard and learned in my boyhood days in Arizona made lasting impressions on me. Many of the things on which I have such strong feelings—feelings which some of my opponents have regarded as unreasonable obsessions—were first impressed on my mind during those early days, and the knowledge I acquired then never left me. On some of those things I believe I am so right in my attitude that I remain uncompromising.

For instance, there is the professional politician. Though I have been in politics for well over forty years, I loathe the professional politician. I have never been a regular. I have fought political machines and party politics at every opportunity. This attitude had its origin in the loudly dressed, slick and sly Indian agents, political appointees, I saw come into Arizona. The first time I ever heard the word politician was at Fort Huachuca, when I was still a small child. The word was applied to those Indian agents. I learned afterwards that they got the jobs because they were small-fry ward heelers. I saw hungry Indians, and the little Indian kids watched us while we munched a Kansas apple or ate a cookie Mother baked. I knew, even as a child, that the government in Washington provided food for all those Indians, but that the "politicians" sold the rations to miners and even to general stores, robbing the

* Miss Lena Coover flew from Los Angeles to New York to attend her former pupil's funeral. *M.R.W.*

Indians of the food the government provided for them. That was my first contact with "politicians."

I had my first experience with a lobby when I was about twelve. My father received a letter from someone in Washington stating that the pay of band leaders could be increased to $100 a month. The pay was then $60 a month. The letter also stated that band leaders could become commissioned officers. I can see the gleam in Dad's eye to this day as he fancied himself adorned with shoulder straps. It all seemed so easy: just sign the agreement to pay one month's salary when the bill became the law, and no further obligation except to send $50 for necessary expenses.

Even as a kid I could not understand this. Why the expenses? There were hints in the letter that it was necessary to see certain Representatives and Senators, and that there were disbursements to be met. It was rather crude. But this technique of the 'nineties didn't differ so much from the technique of our own 'forties. I don't know why, but I felt instinctively that it was wrong. And Mother was on my side. I figured it out that if the men in the various regiments at our post sent in this money, it would amount to $2,250. That was a lot of money in those days. "It's a fake, a swindle," I shouted, and when I ran out of adjectives in denouncing the scheme to my father, I resorted to what to me has always been the most odious thing you could say about people: "They're a bunch of politicians." Father, a musician, who never bothered with politics, was soon talked out of joining the plan. The band leaders of the Army are still waiting for those shoulder straps some of them sent their money to get.

My Arizona days made a lasting impression on me of the "tinhorn" and his ways. Professional gamblers in the West were known as "tinhorns." To me they have been "tinhorns" ever since. But there is one thing that could be said about the professional gambler of over a half century ago in the West: if he was alive, it was a fair assumption that he had not been caught gypping. Gamblers and saloonkeepers were an important part of pioneer Western life, but they were never a reputable part of the community. I remember very well how it used to be said that a gambler or a saloonkeeper could not join the Masons or the Elks. Gamblers were tolerated and patronized but not accepted. If a "tinhorn" in the West was caught cheating, he would never play another game—and there was no coroner's inquest. When I became Mayor of New York, I did my best to make life unpleasant for "tinhorns." They did not have to worry about being shot when caught redhanded, but they were made to fear the law.

My first attempt at applied mathematics—I must have been fourteen or fifteen then—was to figure out the percentage against the player in a crap game, a faro game and what was then called "policy," now known as "the numbers" and other fancy names as well as the old name "policy." Nearly every saloon in Prescott, Arizona, had its gambling department, mainly crap, faro and some Chinese game. There was, of course, a good deal of poker played—not under professional auspices. These games must have been exciting, according to the stories we kids would hear: the guns were laid on the table at easy reach, and of course the games were on the level.

Then "policy" came to town. I remember Mother telling me that it was the same as Lotto, which was sponsored in her native Trieste by the city or the state. Mother would play a ten-cent policy slip almost every week. If she had an exceptional dream, she would risk a quarter. She never won. No one else I knew ever won. The game did not last very long in Prescott and folded up after a few months. I figured it out then as nothing but petty larceny from the pockets of the poor, and showed my mother how she couldn't win.

I was astounded when I finally returned to New York to live in 1906 to find the great influence there of professional gamblers, numbers monarchs, and big "bookies," among others, with close political and judicial connections. They also had many, many friends among the press. I do not mean the reporters. It is easy for this scum of society, these economic vermin, to make friends when they are able to take bets and pay cash if the influential one "happens" to win, and to give unlimited credit if Mr. Big Shot happens to lose. They are no good. They never were any good in Prescott, or New York, and they never will be any good anywhere.

Another early impression that made its mark on my mind was gained from watching the railroad being built between Ashfork, Prescott and Phoenix. There was no machinery used then. It was all manpower and draft animals. The laborers were all immigrants, mostly Mexicans and Italians. If a laborer was injured, he lost his job. If he was killed, no one was notified, because there was no record of his name, address or family. He just had a number. As construction moved on, it left in its wake the injured, the jobless, the stranded victims. Even as a young boy, this struck me as all wrong, and I thought about it a great deal. The more I thought about it, the less able was I to make sense out of that kind of situation. Years later, when I studied law, I learned about such things as "assumed risk," "the fellow servant rule," "contributory negligence," and other similar principles of law, all for the benefit of the employer. I still thought they were all wrong, and later, as a legislator, I did what little I could to have these antiquated eighteenth century rules of law changed. None of them are in use today. Employers' liability, workmen's compensation laws for injury, safeguards against accidents, sanitary and safety laws in factories and for other jobs, unemployment insurance have taken their place. It was this early glimpse of the condition of working people, of their exploitation and their utter lack of protection under the law, which prompted me to take an interest on their side in society. I hope I have made a contribution to progress in this respect.

I remember when the troops were called out to guard the property of the Atlantic & Pacific Railroad during the great Pullman strike of 1894. I was twelve years old then, and it was the first strike I ever knew. I was deeply interested. The whole thing had started with a small group of workers in the bedding department of the Pullman Company, and it spread until it became a general railroad strike throughout the entire country. Even then, as a boy, it occurred to me that surely there should be some way of settling labor disputes of this kind, and that the law should afford equal protection to both sides. I recognized the necessity for President Cleveland's order that there should be no interference with transportation of the United States mail. But I did not quite understand why it was unlawful for employees to inform other employees of grievances, or why they should be kept away from one another by a court mandate, enforced by bayonets of United States soldiers.

These memories were very helpful. It was nearly a life-

time later, as a member of Congress, that I had the opportunity of taking part in preparing the Railways Labor Act
and in the passage of the Norris-La Guardia Anti-injunc-
tion Act. The job is not yet completed. Satisfactory machinery for equitable and just settlement of labor disputes
is still required. I do hope some day to see that job completed.

I also got my first glimpse of racial feeling born of
ignorance, out there in Arizona. I must have been about
ten when a street organ-grinder with a monkey blew into
town. He, and particularly the monkey, attracted a great
deal of attention. I can still hear the cries of the kids: "A
dago with a monkey! Hey, Fiorello, you're a dago too.
Where's your monkey?" It hurt. And what made it worse,
along came Dad, and he started to chatter Neapolitan with
the organ-grinder. He hadn't spoken Italian in many
years, and he seemed to enjoy it. Perhaps, too, he considered the organ-grinder a fellow musician. At any rate,
he promptly invited him to our house for a macaroni dinner. The kids taunted me for a long time after that. I
couldn't understand it. What difference was there between us? Some of their families hadn't been in the country any longer than mine.

I have heard Gilbert and Sullivan's *Pinafore* in almost
every language, in many countries; and in the rendition of
the song, "For He Is an Englishman," the traditional ges-
ture mimicking the organ-grinder and the word "Eyeta-
lian" always annoyed me.

Early in my first administration as Mayor, a traffic
report by the Police Department showed that among the
obstacles to free traffic was the nuisance of the street organ-
grinder. It was with a great deal of gusto that I banned

the organ-grinder from the streets of the City of New York. It caused some resentment among those who were sentimental about organ-grinders. One woman came up to me at a social function and berated me mildly for depriving her of her favorite organ-grinder. "Where do you live?" I asked. "Park Avenue," she said. "What floor?" "The fourteenth," she answered.

In addition to the fact that I never did like organ-grinders ever since my days of ridicule in Prescott when that one organ-grinder came to town, I felt that they made our traffic problem in New York more difficult. I was accused by some New Yorkers who liked them of having no sentimental feelings about organ-grinders, of having no soul, of oppressing the poor, of neglecting more important things to deprive old residents and young children of their pleasure. Some of my correspondents were genial and some were angry. Cornelia Otis Skinner, Beatrice Kauffman, Viola Irene Cooper were among the literary defenders of the hurdy-gurdy. Petitions were got up urging me to rescind the order. My answer to my critics was that there had been a time when the hurdy-gurdy was the only means of bringing music to many people. That was also the time before automobiles filled our streets. With the advent of the phonograph and the radio that time had passed. Free public concerts in parks, libraries, museums and other public places had given ample opportunity to hear music. But, more important, traffic conditions had changed. Children were endangered by trucks and other automobiles when they gathered in the middle of streets to hear and watch the organ-grinders. Also, the simple, sentimental hurdy-gurdy man had become a victim of a racket. My sentimental correspondents did not realize that the Italians' instruments were rented to them by padrones at exorbitant fees. Their licenses from the city were in reality licenses to beg. About a year before I banned the organ-grinders, I had terminated the contracts with musicians on city ferry boats on the grounds that these were merely licenses to beg issued by the city. Despite these reasons, which I gave to my correspondents in answer to their protests, the defenders of the hurdy-gurdy men kept on writing to me for over a year, and some of them warned me that they wouldn't vote again for a man without a soul.

3

The people of the territory of Arizona could not vote in national elections. They had a delegate in the House of Representatives who could talk for them, but who had no vote. In the McKinley-Byran Presidential campaign of 1896, though the people of Arizona could not vote, there was a great deal of campaigning that year for the election of this territorial delegate and for local offices. Arizona, being in the silver belt, leaned toward the Democratic side. The Democrats were then considered the liberal party and the Republicans the conservatives. Like people in all newly settled territory, the people of Arizona leaned toward the so-called liberal side. I was going on fourteen years old now, and this exciting Presidential campaign was the first in which I was able to take interest.

It was during my boyhood in Arizona that I first learned about corrupt local government, and I got my political education from Pulitzer's New York *World*. We had two newspapers in Prescott, the *Journal Miner* and the Prescott *Courier*. These were typical Bret Harte Western newspapers, devoted mostly to local news. When the Sunday edition of the New York *World* arrived in Prescott on the following Friday or Saturday, I would rush to Ross's drugstore where it was on display. There I had looked at the first funny sections I had ever seen, featuring the Yellow Kid. From that comic strip came the expression "yellow journalism." I have enjoyed the comics ever since.

When I got home with the Sunday *World*, I would carefully read every word of the *World*'s fight against the corrupt Tammany machine in New York. That was the period of the lurid disclosures made by the Lexow investigation of corruption in the Police Department that extended throughout the political structure of the city. The papers then were filled with stories of startling crookedness on the part of the police and the politicians in New York. Unlike boys who grew up in the city and who hear from childhood about such things as graft and corruption, the amazing disclosures hit me like a shock. I could not understand how the people of the greatest city in the country could put up with the vice and crime that existed there. A resentment against Tammany was created in me at that time, which I admit is to this day almost an obsession. But I did not become cynical or lose faith in government. I was certain that good people could eliminate bad people from public office. But as I grew older, my hatred of corrupt politicians and my feeling against dishonest and inefficient government increased with the years in proportion with my experience of it.

When I went to live in New York again after my return from Europe in 1906, Tammany was once more all-powerful. It was the era of "honest graft." When I had to choose a political party, my choice was easy. I joined the Republican Party. I was young and innocent. A party in the minority cannot help being good and pure. That seemed the only avenue I could choose at the time in order to carry out my boyhood dreams of going to work against corrupt government.

4

There was, of course, great excitement at Whipple Barracks in Prescott when the news reached us that the U.S. battleship *Maine* had been blown up in the harbor of Havana, Cuba, on the fifteenth of February 1898. The Postal Telegraph operator in Prescott pasted up Associated Press bulletins on the *Maine* disaster as soon as they came in, and along with the other children of Army men, as well as the parents, I watched and waited eagerly for the latest news. We expected war momentarily, especially after the news came that two hundred and fifty American lives had been lost.

Within about ten days, orders came for our regiment to get itself ready for war. Inventories were taken. The equipment of some other regiments and of National Guard units was not up to date, but our regiment had the modern Krag-Jörgensen rifles. Some of our noncommissioned officers had seen service in the Civil War.

As the weeks passed and there was still no declaration of war, there was a feeling in our military circles that President McKinley was hesitating too long. But it finally came on April twenty-fifth, and our regiment was soon sent to Jefferson Barracks, St. Louis, Missouri. It remained there for a few days and then went into camp at Mobile, Alabama, but the families of the officers and enlisted men remained in quarters at Jefferson Barracks.

Though I was only fifteen years old, I was restless and wanted to join the Army. My age, and the fact that I was short and under the required weight, made that impossible. But I persuaded the St. Louis *Post-Dispatch* to pay my fare to the camp at Mobile where my father was stationed. I did a couple of articles for the *Post-Dispatch* from the camp.

As an Army child I was familiar with drill and other training courses. I noticed at that time that it was very difficult to train Army officers quickly, though it was easy to train a large body of men in a hurry once you had the officers to do the job. This knowledge was very useful to me later when I was a legislator, and particularly when I became a member of the House Committee on Military Affairs. I also noticed at that time that the Medical Corps was both inefficient and insufficient in the Spanish-American War. During the first world war the Medical Corps brought its technique and efficiency almost to perfection. In the second world war it surpassed anything that had been attained previously in this and, perhaps, in any other country. But the government's record as a whole during the Spanish-American War was not up to the heroism of our men who took part in that war.

My particular Spanish-American War hero was "Bucky" O'Neil. I remember that he came to our school soon after the declaration of war and told us what that declaration meant, and what war meant. He expressed the opinion that when we won this war, no other nation would ever again attempt to dominate territory in the Western Hemisphere. When Arizona provided a troop for Colonel Theodore Roosevelt's Rough Riders, "Bucky" O'Neil became a member of that troop. I felt he should have commanded it. He was killed in action during the famous charge on San Juan Hill.

One of the worst scandals of our entire military history occurred during this short Spanish-American War and made a lasting impresssion upon me, for my father was one of its victims. Corrupt contractors supplied the Army with diseased beef. My father became so ill as a result of eating some of this diseased beef that he had to be discharged from the service on account of disability. Though we did not know it then, he had only a few years to live because of the work of crooked Army contractors.

That experience never left my mind. When I became a Congressman during World War I, the first measure I introduced in the House was a bill providing the death penalty for contractors who supplied defective food or other supplies and equipment in time of war, and a heavy jail sentence, if they sold such stuff in time of peace. I introduced that measure on April 3, 1917, a few days before Congress declared war on Germany. It was referred to the Committee on Judiciary, where it was allowed to languish. But I still think it is a good idea. It might prevent other families from losing their fathers.

After Father's discharge from the Army, our family returned to New York City, where we renewed old acquaintances. Then the family went to Trieste, to live with my mother's family. It was while we were in Trieste that my father died in 1901, a victim of condemned Army meat.

CHAPTER II

Consular Service

1

AFTER MY FAMILY moved to Trieste, all we had to live on was my father's small pension from the Army. I had to get a job. Raymond Willey, American Consular Agent in Fiume, got me a job as clerk in the American consulate in Budapest. Although the government did not pay me much of a salary, it was a good opportunity to learn useful things and gain valuable experience.

Frank Dyer Chester, of Boston, was the Consul General at Budapest. He was most helpful in guiding me in my studies, particularly in the study of languages. My ears were accustomed to Italian, and the smattering of Latin I had picked up in school made the Italian language comparatively easy, but I began to study it and German systematically. Mr. Chester did me a good turn by sending me to Croatia one summer for four months for the express purpose of studying Croatian. Croatian was tough, with its seven cases, all of them used, and its many conjugations of verbs. While I never pretended to be expert in this language, I did learn enough of it to pass a Civil Service examination later, which enabled me to get the job as interpreter at Ellis Island that helped me work my way through law school.

Mr. Chester was not a politician. He was a scholarly

gentleman who had won honors at Harvard, including a post-graduate scholarship which sent him to the Near East for his doctoral thesis. He was a master linguist and knew Arabic, Assyrian and other Semitic languages. He also had a thorough knowledge of Hungarian. He was one of the few Americans who ever mastered that difficult language. I never could, or even seriously tried.

Mr. Chester had obtained his consular appointment because of his Harvard connections, and through the influence of Senator Henry Cabot Lodge, of Massachusetts. He never was able to forget that he was a Harvard man, and he solemnly assured me that because I did not have a degree from Harvard I would never get any higher than the menial position of clerk in the American foreign service. There were not many career men in the service in the early nineteen hundreds. There was no tenure of office provided by law. Today the Foreign Service has been established on a more orderly and permanent basis and has become a regular career, with regular promotions for merit, tenure of office established by law, and pensions on retirement. The Foreign Service consists of a fine body of conscientious and talented public officers. Though there are still some political appointments made by the President, these are mainly at the very top level of ambassadors and ministers. Some of the political appointments during the past thirteen years have not been so good.

I devoted a good deal of my spare time while in the Consular Service to the study of history as well as languages. I laid a groundwork then that was very useful to me later. I kept informed about current events at home by reading every newspaper and magazine I could lay my hands on.

My duties at Budapest were chiefly making out consular invoices, taking applications for visas and American passports, and acting as what our consul loved to call "amanuensis." We had no typewriters in the consulate, and I had to do all the copying by hand from scribbled notes made by Mr. Chester. I also gathered information and compiled statistics for the quarterly and annual reports of the Consul General.

2

Budapest was at the height of its glory in those ten years before the first world war smashed the Austro-Hungarian Empire forever. One could hear more good music in Budapest in 1902 and 1903 than in Vienna. The town was considered the gayest in Europe, and many American dancers and other entertainers turned up there. Our duties at the consulate brought us into contact with these people.

My first and only extra-consular reward was a big kiss from Loie Fuller, famous for her "Serpentine dance" at the Chicago World's Fair. Loie Fuller was in Budapest on her way to dance in Russia. One day I was sent to her hotel with her passport. A cocktail party was in progress when I arrived. It was the first cocktail party I had seen in my nineteen years of existence. Loie Fuller invited me in and asked me to have a drink. I did not drink at that age. She asked me a few questions about myself and thanked me for her passport. Then she bent down and gave me a big kiss, and I went away very happy.

Another of our well-known visitors was Isadora Duncan. She was a great artist, but she always seemed to manage to get into a great deal of trouble. One of the jobs assigned to me by the Consul General was to placate Isadora's "reader." He recited poetry while she danced, and he was deeply offended when the local papers criticized his work. He walked out on Isadora, and the consul told me to stick with him until I had persuaded him to go back to work. I rode around Budapest all day long with this temperamental individual and listened patiently to his accounts of how misunderstood and unappreciated he was. At first, he would not hear of working with Isadora again, claiming that she, too, had hurt his feelings. But I convinced him without too much trouble, though it did take a good deal of time, that he was indispensable to Isadora. He agreed to go back, if she would come out on the stage and take a bow with him, holding his hand. Isadora consented to the terms. But she managed to give him a shove that almost made him lose his balance before the audience and nearly precipitated the whole quarrel over again.

Among the many vaudeville performers, musicians, actors and actresses who passed through the Budapest consulate was a bleached blonde. Mr. Chester warned me and Paul Tomanoczy, who also worked as a clerk at the consulate, that if he caught us going out with her, he would fire us at once. That was enough for us, so that evening we called at the actress' hotel and took her to the Folies Bergeres. Mr. Chester must have suspected us, for he appeared at the theatre, too, and promptly fired us. But we soon persuaded Mr. Gerster, the Vice Consul, to get him to hire us back again. Mr. Chester had the right idea, however, for the blonde proved to be well known for blackmail.

I got my first taste of the bewildering continental code of sophisticated domestic manners while I was a young clerk in the Budapest consulate. At a party one day, one of the guests pointed out another guest and said to me: "He is very jealous of that young Hussar officer, and I am very troubled. He's my superior in our bureau." I saw that the young Hussar was talking animatedly with a very handsome lady. "Who is she?" I asked, glancing in the direction of the lady in the case. "She is my wife," he answered. I went away quite confused.

3

When Raymond Willey, who had got me the job as clerk in Budapest, went back to the United States to become associated with the Harbison-Walker Refractories Company, manufacturers of fireproof bricks, of which he later became president, he got me his post as Consular Agent in Fiume. Since I was not yet twenty-one, I could serve only as Acting Consular Agent until February 1904 when my commission, signed by Secretary of State John Hay, was sent to me.

When I took over the office in Fiume, I had no assistance and acted as boss, clerk and my own messenger. On several occasions I had to make decisions which would have got me into trouble had I guessed wrong. My salary was the munificent sum of $800 a year. The law provided that certain posts were paid out of the consular fees collected. But if my fees at the minor post in Fiume ever exceeded a thousand dollars in any one year, the government took the balance. But, at least, I was sure of my $66 a month. I got along all right financially. My $800 was equal to four thousand crowns, and I managed to hold my own socially with the local government officials and junior Army officers with whom I associated. That was all that was expected of me. Of course, I could not afford to gamble or indulge in many of the popular vices—an indulgence which got many of our young Foreign Service officers into trouble. When it was all over, I just about broke even. I had no debts, and I had no cash.

I had only taken over my post a short time when I had my first important diplomatic case. Anything concerning the rights of American citizens under treaties between the United States and Hungary was considered diplomatic. Routine matters, such as consular invoices and bills of health for ships clearing Fiume for United States ports, were consular affairs.

It was Corpus Christi Day, a national holiday in Hungary. Fiume was at that time an autonomous city of the Hungarian crown. The Catholic religion was the state religion. As on all national holidays, foreign consuls displayed the flags of their respective nations. My office was on the Corso, the main street of Fiume. As a regiment of Hungarian troops filed down the Corso, the Stars and Stripes attracted the attention of one soldier, a coal miner from Scranton, Pennsylvania, who had been grabbed and drafted into the Hungarian Army while he was on a vacation, visiting his parents. When he saw the flag, he told me later, he suddenly thought: "What am I doing here? I am an American citizen." That evening he came around to the consulate. It was after office hours, but I happened to be in, for my living quarters were in the same apartment as the office. There were two rooms, one the consulate of the United States of America, the other my bedroom. There was no bathroom. That was a community affair in the hallway, like our old-law tenements in New York.

The soldier, still in his uniform, was quite timid. He asked to see the consul, and I told him he was looking at him. He seemed surprised, but I assured him I was it. Then he told me his story, which was quite typical of all our "military cases." We had had quite a few similar ones while I was a clerk in Budapest. This soldier had gone to America when he was in his teens, worked in the coal mines, become an American citizen, saved his money and paid a visit to the old folks at home in Hungary, with the intention, too, of marrying his boyhood sweetheart and taking her back to America with him. There were not many Croatian women in the United States at that time, and most of the industrious, hardworking boys who became American citizens went back to their native land to marry and then returned to the United States to raise big American families. My contact at an early age with some of these people made it impossible for me to understand the kind of prejudice and even hatred of immigrants that was so prevalent in this country. After all, did not every one of us descend from immigrant stock? Some arrived on the *Mayflower* and many more in the steerage.

This soldier, whose name, I believe, was Kovacevic, had not been in his native village long when he was nabbed and kept in the cooler until the military called for him, put him in uniform and made him a soldier of His Apostolic Majesty's Army. He had refused to sign a disclaimer of American citizenship when requested to do so, and had registered his protest, to which no attention was paid. I asked to see his citizenship papers. The sheriff had taken them away from him when he was arrested, and he had never seen them again. I questioned him closely to make sure that he had obtained final citizenship papers. We had many cases where only first papers, or declarations of intention to become citizens, had been obtained, and these people were not protected under our treaty with Hungary. I was convinced that Kovacevic was a full American citizen and had not been called into military service before emigrating, which was another of the provisions of the treaty.

I proceeded at once to draft a protest to the Hungarian government and demanded the immediate release from the Hungarian Army of this sovereign American citizen. I called on the appropriate civil official that same evening and personally delivered the protest to him, plus a stump speech in which I quoted all the precedents under the treaty which I knew and had memorized. I could rattle them off glibly, and I injected a big dose of one celebrated case about a Hussar, which may or may not have had anything to do with this particular case. This was my first "diplomatic case" on my own, and I gave it the works.

Fortunately, the Hungarian official was experienced, had seen long service and was quite familiar with such matters. He assured me that he would immediately transmit the case to the Ministry and would keep me informed. I then asked for the release of the soldier pending consideration of the case, for I did not want him transferred to another regiment at some distance, in the meantime. This was something new, but I was promised that the civil official would take the matter up informally with the regimental commander. I was bluffing on that one, for I had not yet legally established the soldier's American citizenship. Much to my surprise, the soldier was in my office next day, all smiles, with a ten-day leave of absence. And, once his citizenship papers were obtained and the date of his emigration verified, there was no trouble getting his final discharge with official expressions of regret for the action of the minor, local officials, unfamiliar with treaty provisions.

Then I made my report to the Consul General at Budapest and awaited the commendation I thought I had earned. Imagine my disappointment when instead I received a strong reprimand for having taken up the case before reporting the facts to the Consul General and getting his instructions to act. By that time the soldier might have disappeared into another part of the country or another regiment. I did as told thereafter, but I was glad that I had managed to rescue one American citizen from the clutches of Hungarian recruiting officers all on my own.

4

During my three years in Fiume, I not only met many interesting people, but I had a chance to observe situations, locally troublesome then, which later became matters of international importance. The Croatians with whom I came into contact at this time hated the Hungarian government passionately. They had every reason to do so. The Hapsburg policy was the age-old one of Divide and Conquer. It was put into practice every day before my eyes. Antagonisms and hatreds were carefully and systematically engendered. The Croatians were brought up to hate the Serbians and trained and aided by the government in that hatred. All of the South Slavic groups were kept at one another's throats. Any sensible person could see the devastating effect of this unchristian, inhuman system of teaching people to hate one another. The Serbians, Croatians, Dalmatians, Bosnians, Herzegovinians,

Montenegrins, Slovenes, all similarly exploited, all kept in the same abject poverty, were stimulated to take their hatreds out on one another instead of their exploiters. Their only real difference was that some of them were communicants of the Roman Catholic Church and others of the Greek Orthodox Church. Both these churches had practically the same beliefs and dogmas. And the Hapsburg politicians kept up a constant instigation among all of them to hate their neighbors, the Italians. It is no wonder that after centuries of such influences there is misunderstanding and lack of harmony among these people, who have finally been brought together under one government.

The same tactics, the same intrigues, were practiced by larger nations, I have since noticed. For reasons I could never understand some nations would like to see internecine strife continue in the Balkans. The people of the United States have never been familiar with the political background of these unhappy people of southeastern Europe. Even with some knowledge of their history and past sufferings, it is difficult enough to understand these complex relationships and the conditions existing in these countries.

There never seemed to me any good reason why the Italians and the Yugoslavs could not get along together. The two adjoining countries could well supplement each other's native products. Both peoples are romantic, love music, base their society on the institutions of the family; both are God-loving, religious people. Understanding cannot be brought about overnight. At best, it will take a long time to overcome the antagonisms so successfully stimulated by their unsuccessful, departed rulers.

Neither Great Britain, which has used the old Hapsburg policy of Divide and Conquer, nor our own government has been helpful in overcoming these antagonisms. At times our own Embassy at Belgrade has been guilty of the most unpardonable kind of intrigue and has engaged in the worst kind of propaganda. In recent times I have seen the evidence. Had it not been for the unfortunate viewpoint and reprehensible conduct of the men first sent there by our government following the end of World War II, the United States would have had tremendous influence in Yugoslavia. Our representatives not only created strained relations among factions and groups, but, what is more deplorable, they destroyed the unquestioning, almost childlike, faith, love and affection which the people of Yugoslavia had, and want to have, for Americans.

The various Slavic elements in this part of the world where I gained my first practical experience of foreign affairs will get along after hereditary memories are dimmed. But these people must be given a chance and time to forget as well as to learn. It took about seventy years to soften the feeling between the North and the South in these United States after the Civil War, and there are still a few scars that have not been fully healed. We were at odds for only four years. In the old Austro-Hungarian Empire a series of wars down through the last three centuries has heightened racial antagonisms and increased national prejudices.

5

My life in Fiume was not all consular invoices, diplomatic cases and study of racial and national antagonisms.

I had time for a few scrapes of my own, and the most amusing was my duel.

Carnival season was joyously observed in this Adriatic region. There were parades, parties and masked balls; and happy revelry at this season amounted to a tradition. Rich and poor, young and old, took part in the festivities. Certain customs were carefully observed, and disregard of any of the rules constituted a serious social offense, which was never overlooked or condoned.

There was a series of week-end balls with very low admission prices. The official Elite Ball took place on the last Sunday before Mardi Gras. At this Elite Ball the ladies all wore costumes and were masked. Some of the men wore masquerade costumes and were required to act out the role and to speak the particular dialect of the characters they were impersonating. It was the ladies' privilege to make the first approach to the men. Considering the many inhibitions imposed by custom on the girls the rest of the time, it was only fair that at least once a year it should be permissible for them to talk to young men without formal introductions, and without Mama being present. At the Elite Ball there was much decorum and plenty of philandering. Many happy and serious love affairs started at these functions. The code was severe and required the most gentlemanly conduct toward the masked lady and full protection for her. This code was strictly adhered to by all social classes. Once in a while there was a bit of disappointment when a man found he had been dining and wining his own wife. And sometimes some skillful detective work was carried on by jealous wives.

I shall never forget the first masked ball I attended in Fiume. I was rigged out in tails and white tie. I felt just as uncomfortable as I always do when I wear that silly costume. I was approached by a masked girl with a lovely figure, who wore a very elegant costume. She addressed me by name, and we danced. After a dance, the gentleman was not permitted to excuse himself if the lady desired to continue in his company. It was quite proper, however, for another masked lady to "cut in," and then the gentleman made the decision.

The young lady who approached me had a sweet voice, and it was apparent that she was cultured. She dropped many little hints which indicated that she was familiar with my work. We were "cut in" on a few times, but she managed to come back, so that at intermission time she was with me. I had been properly briefed on procedure, and I knew that the next move was mine. I asked her to dine with me, and the invitation was accepted. At eleven-thirty, the proper time to leave, we got our coats. It was the custom not to return to this swanky ball but to give one's return check to someone outside waiting to get in. After intermission the party was for the hoi polloi, and then it sometimes got a bit rough.

The young lady and I started down the Corso, and there my trouble began. The sidewalk was packed with couples, merry and noisy. Suddenly we were approached by a gentleman in evening clothes, who said to my companion: "Albina, I will not stand for this!" "I beg your pardon, sir, you have made a mistake, please go your own way," she answered, and, turning to me, said, "I wish to remain with you." The irate intruder then made a thrust in an attempt to pull off her mask. That was an unpardonable violation of the rules. I don't remember whether I knew that particular rule, but I did feel that I owed the lady protection, and so I instantly shot a right hook to the gentleman's chin, which accidentally landed properly, caught him off balance, and he sprawled in the street. The crowd around us, who witnessed the whole affair cheered. He picked himself up and rushed at me with an uplifted cane, which grazed my shoulder. I grabbed it and broke it across my knee. Then the men, leaving their lady companions, rushed the poor fellow, and I had to go to his rescue. By that time the cops had arrived. The whole crowd protested against my assailant's actions, and he was roughly pushed out of the crowd by the local gendarmes.

My companion and I dined together and had a merry time. By the time we had finished, the crowd had had sufficient liquid stimulation to become "crowd silly," and I was a big shot in their eyes because of this encounter. At the appointed time, the ladies had five minutes in which to leave. If they chose to remain, they were required to unmask. My sweet companion left. It was highly improper to follow or attempt to identify her.

I thought no more about the incident. Three days later a young lady came to my office. She introduced herself as the sister of the jealous young man who had started the fracas. She was a young teacher in the primary grades. Her brother was the main support of their widowed mother. He was a telegraph operator and a reserve officer in His Majesty's Army. The young lady of the mask who had been my companion was also a telegraphist. He was madly in love with her. She, in turn, was trifling with his affections, and the sister's story went on and on, until I asked, "Well, what is it I can do?" "Only you can save my brother his job," she answered. "How?" "Well, it is this way: he was struck by you; being an Army officer he cannot take such an affront and is required to demand satisfaction." I still did not get it. I assured the solicitous sister that I had no intention of stealing his girl. No, that was not it. Unless her brother challenged me to a duel, he would lose his reserve commission and his dismissal from the Royal Post and Telegraph Service would follow as a matter of course.

"Well, why doesn't he challenge me?" I asked. I really had not given the subject any thought when I blurted that out. Ah, that was the whole trouble, the sister explained. Had he challenged me in time, within twenty-four hours, he would have been completely in order and in the clear. Then it would have been up to me. But, since he had failed to send his seconds within the time limit, would I please be so kind and considerate, for the mother's sake, not to raise the question of the time limit and thus save her brother from lifetime disqualification as a gentleman, in addition to loss of his job? "Sure," I said. "Now what do I do?" Nothing at all, she explained. When his seconds called, I was merely to say nothing about the time having expired. I assured the young lady that I would not be the cause of her mother's son losing his job, though I failed to see where I came into this mess. She was most grateful and appreciative. She had been crying, but she cheered up. I realized that the family was much distressed, funny as the whole thing might be from my American point of view.

I now was able to identify my masked companion. I had met her when I went to the telegraph office to send messages to the Consulate General in Budapest. She was talented as well as beautiful.

It was hardly an hour after the unhappy sister had left,

much relieved, when two young men paid me a call. They wore top hats, Prince Albert coats, were properly gloved and caned. They told me they represented the gentleman in question, whose name I have forgotten. I had insulted their principal in a manner unbecoming a gentleman. Would I be good enough to name my seconds? Physical violence having occurred, their principal having actually been struck, the offense demanded a settlement on the "field of honor." "What's that?" I asked. "A duel," they replied. "The seconds will duly select the weapons, the time and the place." They then told me the time would be tomorrow morning and would I be good enough to name my seconds? I thought the whole thing was pretty silly, but I had promised the young sister that I would not permit her brother to lose his job on my account. It then suddenly dawned on me that I might lose mine for being engaged in such a ridiculous performance.

Well, I named my seconds. One was a Mr. Radmonovic, who was head of the Royal Hungarian tobacco monopoly in Fiume. He was a fine, most serious gentleman and had been a good friend of my predecessor and was a good friend of mine. He helped us both in our German, which he spoke perfectly. The other second I named was the Turkish Consul, who was a rogue. I selected him for the fun of it. He was a notorious roué, had married an old and ugly widow with plenty of money, and his chief mission in life was spending her money on other women. That is how we became friends—aside from our formal official contacts—for he swiped a girl from me, a singer in light opera. My $800 a year could not compete with his wife's millions. The old effendi was a card, and he was much amused when I told him the story, and, of course, consented to act in this "affair of honor."

The seconds arranged to get together promptly. I was told to remain in readiness, and that I would be informed that evening where and when I would be wanted. In the meantime, I got hold of an old pal of mine, Lieutenant Karl Selak, of the 79th Infantry Regiment, a fine fellow, always broke, always being chased by creditors. At least once a month Karl was ordered to arrange some settlement with his creditors or commit suicide. That was also part of the Hungarian Army officer's code. Only a dead officer was permitted to default on his debts. Lieutenant Selak and I used to walk together, run around the long break-water together and row together. He had also given me a few lessons in fencing. I was not good at it and did not have enough interest to stick at it and practice.

Off Karl and I went to the garrison gym. All afternoon he coached me in lunges and thrusts with a sword. It seemed reasonably certain that our duel would be with swords. Our bellies and throats would be bandaged for protection. At least, that was the way Karl Selak doped it out. By the time he was through describing the procedure to me I was really worried. We considered our plan of attack. At the word go I was to spring an *ausschlag:* "down full left swing and thrust for the head." Since my knowledge of fencing was so limited, I would have to draw first blood, which in all likelihood would end the affair, or else I might be in danger of getting hurt, for I was very poor on the defensive.

When Selak thought I had had enough practice, we quit and went to the Café Grande for our five o'clock "mé-lange." It was there that my second Radmonovic came and told me to be ready at five o'clock the next morning. He would meet me right there at the same table in that same café. The details had not yet been worked out, but the seconds would meet again that evening. The duel would take place on the breakwater, behind the boathouse. The weapons, in all probability, would be swords. Pistols had already been ruled out. My offense warranted pistols, but inasmuch as I had been so chivalrous about waiving the time limit, my opponent would "gallantly" waive his choice of weapons, and my seconds would therefore have the choice.

Meanwhile, Karl Selak did his work. He passed the word on to the junior officers who generally met with the young civil officials, about my great skill as a fencer, giving me a big, false build-up. That maneuver worked all right.

That night Selak and I dined together and went to a cheap café chantant afterwards, the only one playing at the time. I could not have slept anyhow, so we remained out quite late. Long after midnight, we played billiards at one of the all-night cafés. I did get a couple of hours sleep and arrived at the Grande late, the last one to turn up.

The four seconds were there, as well as my "antagonist," who looked quite confident to me. Karl Selak had told me not to eat anything, and so I ordered some black coffee. He assured me that I would get food at the hospital afterwards.

Everybody stood up. We bowed to one another, and all sat down again. The waiter brought my coffee. The others had theirs. Then Radmonovic, my second, pulled out a lengthy document, written in both Italian and Hungarian. It had several sheets of text, closely written in longhand. I was told to sign it. I think I signed at least three times. Then the other fellow was told to sign. Then we were told to shake hands. We did. Then the seconds all shook hands. Then we shook hands with the seconds. Then Radmonovic ordered cognacs for all. That was for a bracer. I gobbled mine down and asked where we were to go. "Home," said Radmonovic, "it's all over." "What?" I asked, surprised. Yes, he told me, the seconds had agreed that the conduct of the challenger had been highly improper, that there was ample proof that I had not struck him until he gave me reason to believe that he was attempting to lift the mask of my companion, which he really did not attempt to do, but his action had justified the belief that he would have done so. The "jury of honor" had also found that I had not intentionally departed from "conduct becoming a gentleman," but had naturally resented the "affront," in keeping with the custom of my country, which country had not adopted the code of honor prevalent in Hungary and most "cultured countries." The jury of honor had decided that the whole affair was an unfortunate incident, and that, moreover, the lady in question was entitled to protection, which I had properly given to her. They also found that the challenger, having realized his mistake, had, in keeping with the accepted conduct, acted in a manner befitting a gentleman of honor and an officer in His Majesty's Army. There was, therefore, no valid reason why the controversy should be continued, each of the parties having honorably explained his conduct to the full and complete satisfaction of the jury of honor. That was the end of my first and only duel. Albina, the cause of it, and I became good friends. I introduced her to Radmonovic, and some years later they were married.

6

When I went to Fiume in the autumn of 1903, the Cunard Line had just opened a semi-monthly passenger service between Fiume and New York. Four slow-speed steamers were put into this service. As no one in the Budapest office had had any experience with immigrants to America, I had to start from scratch. I read everything we had about immigration, including the quarantine regulations and the duties required of consular officers dealing with immigrants. The laws, rules and regulations were not annotated, and there was very little in our limited library on the subject. But I did gather that I had to "certify to the health of all passengers and crews and give the ship a certificate that it had cleared from a port free from contagious diseases or illnesses subject to quarantine regulations and that bedding and other household goods had been properly fumigated." I learned that the passengers were required to go aboard ship as late as possible before actual sailing time. But the rules and regulations made no mention of specific duties of consular officers stationed at ports of embarkation and placed on them no definite responsibilities in connection with immigrants and the process of immigration. Only in the quarantine regulations was it suggested that consular officers should "ascertain" the facts concerning the health of the passengers and crews of departing ships and should be "satisfied" that conditions and facts were in keeping with the certificates they issued.

It occurred to me that with so many causes for exclusion of immigrants and so many restrictions on their entry into the United States, it was strange that there should be no definite provision for inquiry, investigation and check-up in the country of origin or at the port of embarkation, where accurate information was available. I discussed this situation with my immediate superior, the Consul General, who agreed with me that I could retain physicians to inspect immigrants at the time of their embarkation. He also agreed that since anyone afflicted with a contagious or loathsome disease was inadmissible under our immigration laws, such persons could be prevented from sailing under the more explicit regulations of the Quarantine Law.

Being new at Fiume, I took a look around and decided to retain a certain resident practicing physician who had a good reputation and took an interest in public health matters. I found him to be quite interested in the subject and that he had given it a great deal of thought. He told me that he had been particularly concerned about the local health of a small community like Fiume in relation to the constant flow of large numbers of transients into the town, on their way to America. The population of Fiume in 1903-1906 was only about 30,000, and the estimated number of emigrants was 2,500 a month.

The day of the sailing of an emigrant ship arrived soon after I became Acting Consular Agent. About eighty emigrants were to embark, and I was invited to "tea" on board ship. I cannot describe the surprise and consternation of the Cunard officials when I arrived with my doctor and inquired about the health of the passengers. To say that the representatives of the steamship company were horrified is putting it mildly. The local Hungarian authorities were just confused. They, like myself, had no previous experience in these matters.

The Cunard officials insisted vigorously that I had no

authority to inspect emigrants, told me that they had been carrying passengers to America since before I was born, and stated flatly that they would not permit either my doctor or myself to "look at an emigrant." The Hungarian officials said that if it were possible to detect anyone who would be inadmissible before he sailed, they could not see why it was not the humane thing to do.

I left the ship, and a few minutes after I got back to my office on the Corso, a clerk came for the Bill of Health with the five dollar fee required for it. I refused to issue the Bill of Health. The Cunard officials soon realized, for the first time apparently, that I meant business. The captain of the ship was worried. He came to the consulate personally to protest, but he remained to plead with me. I told him that if he would disembark the emigrants and permit me to examine them, I would be glad to do so, but that if he did not consent to that, I would insist on disinfecting the entire ship. He asked for an hour's time, and we went back to the ship together.

The emigrants were all on deck. I examined each one of them with my doctor and stamped their cards, while the Cunard representative and the British Consul filed a formal protest against my action. They paid the fee for the Bill of Health but refused to pay my doctor's fee. They claimed that for me to demand that they pay the doctor was "adding insult to injury." I was not worried about that. I knew that another ship was coming along soon. When that ship arrived, I made them pay the doctor's fee for the previous ship, the *Aurania*, and deposit enough money to pay for the doctor's fee on the second ship. They had to do it to get clearance, but they did it all under protest, pending a decision from Washington on my ruling.

Before long there was complete cooperation on the part of the steamship line, and we had a smaller percentage of rejections for health at Ellis Island than any other port in the world. The routine became well established. Inspection was speedy and efficient, and we saved many hundreds of innocent people from the expense of taking a trip all the way to New York only to be found inadmissible on health grounds and sent back.

Washington never gave a decision on whether I was right or wrong in my interpretation of the regulations and my insistence on prior physical examinations before sailing. But I kept right on with the practice, and many years afterwards I learned that the Public Health Service as well as the Immigration Service were greatly interested in my innovation. Fiume was the only port where emigrants were inspected before embarkation. During my time there, from 1903 to 1906, we must have inspected at least eighty to ninety thousand of them.

Twenty-five years later it was a source of great satisfaction to me to see a bill presented to Congress by the Department of Labor asking that such examinations as I had instituted be made mandatory all over the world. Public Health Service doctors were assigned to ports of embarkation to give the examinations. The system should have been a source of satisfaction to the steamship lines, too, and was of great importance to the poor emigrants, for in the three years of my service at Fiume we had only forty-five emigrants rejected for trachoma, while the average rejection for that disease from other ports was about twenty-five for each ship reaching the United States.

The examination of emigrants at the scene of their boarding ship was picturesque and created quite a lot of interest and excitement in the small port city of Fiume. Each emigrant carried his bag, crammed with all his worldly goods; the children tagged along behind their parents. They all walked up to a platform, stepped up to a doctor, who examined them for physical defects, took their temperature and then passed them on to the next doctor for examination of their eyes for trachoma, which was the most prevalent infectious disease at the time. The thousands of emigrants rejected every year at Ellis Island because of trachoma went back to their native lands disappointed, heartbroken, "broke," for they had sold all their property and taken all their savings to pay for their passage to the land of hope.

At Fiume we protected the emigrants from all persons not officially concerned with them. They were met at the train and taken to an emigrant hostelry until time to go aboard ship. As they embarked, we examined about two hundred of them an hour. The time for their boarding ship was fixed as close as practicable before sailing time, so that they would not be kept in their close quarters on shipboard any longer than necessary. Sometimes we had as many as two thousand departing on one ship, and the average was between a thousand and fifteen hundred a voyage in those years when immigration was unrestricted.

The sight of emigrants embarking got to be not only popular, but fashionable. Big shots would obtain permits from the Hungarian officials to watch the scene, and there would often be as many as thirty or forty visitors. They would stand on the first-class deck where they could get a gallery view of the entire procedure. There were always some socially prominent people and high government officials among the visitors.

On one occasion I got into quite a controversy as a result of this practice of going to see the "interesting" emigrants. The S.S. *Panonia* was in port, and she was scheduled to sail on the following Saturday. About Tuesday or Wednesday, I received word from the steamship agent that there would be an embarkation of emigrants that afternoon. I asked if the sailing date had been changed and was informed that it had not. This embarkation was to be a "command performance." Her Imperial Highness the Archduchess Maria Josefa was visiting the city of Fiume and had expressed a desire to see an embarkation. I sent word back that I regretted very much that it could not be done, for the emigrants could not be kept on board ship at the dock for three days without danger to their health. The U.S. quarantine regulations required that steerage passengers board a ship as close as possible to sailing time, and I could not possibly stretch that time to three full days and nights. Word came back that His Excellency the Governor General had ordered the embarkation, that the time for it had been fixed and could not now be changed. "Sorry," I replied, but I would not approve it and would not attend.

I was visited by the senior Hungarian official in charge of the port. He explained that the situation would permit of no alteration, told me how important it was, and assured me that I would be given the great honor of having tea with Her Imperial Highness on board ship. It was just a demonstration, he told me. It would only be necessary to inspect two hundred emigrants, as it would be too tiring for Her Highness to watch any more. "No, it can not be done," I insisted. I was then politely told that embarkation would take place as planned by the Hungarian officials, and that was all there was to it. I was also told that, if I did not attend, it would be an affront to Her Imperial Highness which His Majesty's government could not overlook, and that the government would be reluctantly compelled to request my recall. He bowed and departed.

I knew that he intended to go through with it and embark the passengers. I then wrote the master of the ship, Captain Pentecoste, a fine sailor gentleman, called his attention to our quarantine regulations and informed him that if he took on passengers three days before sailing time, I would not issue the Bill of Health required before his ship could enter the port of New York. I also pointed out that under the law a heavy fine and long quarantine period were the penalties for any ship seeking to clear without a Bill of Health.

The captain decided not to take any such chance, and messages began to fly back and forth thick and fast between the Governor General's office and the American consulate. Messengers arrived at my room with important-looking statements, some of them appeals, some of them threats. I realized that the best thing I could do was to make myself scarce. So as the middle of the afternoon had arrived, I took a long walk and dropped in rather early for tea with a friend, a place where I could call without a formal invitation. My hostess played the piano well; we chatted, and I stayed there until dark and then left, for I knew that by that time the storm must have blown over. I had dinner that night at the home of the British Consul. He had been on board the ship during the afternoon to take tea with Her Imperial Highness and His Excellency the Governor General. They had roasted me alive. I had affronted a member of the Imperial family; I was rude and discourteous. They had been looking everywhere for me, and everyone at the British Consul's home that night wondered how I could hide in the small town of Fiume without being found. The officer in charge of the port had been sent to locate me, and the British Consul told me how embarrassed that officer was when he had to report back every twenty minutes or so that he was unable to find the American Consul. There wasn't any mystery about it. If he had only known, I was having tea at his own home with his wife. I think a complaint was filed against me in Washington, but I never heard anything on that one either. But I did miss meeting Her Imperial Highness.

After three years in the Consular Service, I got restless and was anxious to return home, where I could continue my education and make a better career for myself. I had made up my mind that three years in Fiume would be enough, for I had a great deal to learn before I could acquire anything like a good education. I felt that the life I was leading was too easy. Too much of the time I had nothing to do. I wanted more action, and I did not see any future for myself in diplomacy. Taking stock of myself, I realized that I had a good command of languages, but no money. I also realized that it was not good for a young and ambitious American to remain in that service too long at a time. There was the danger of becoming self-satisfied, not too industrious, and of acquiring too much of a taste for idle social life. I handed in my resignation. After it was accepted, I had to pay for my passage home by working on a British ship. I acted as interpreter and assisted the ship's doctor in vaccinating eighteen hundred emigrants on board.

CHAPTER III

Ellis Island

1

W<small>HEN</small> I <small>RETURNED</small> to New York in 1906 after resigning from the Consular Service, I had a definite plan worked out in my mind for my future. I wanted first to complete my education, get admitted to the bar and then enter public service. Raymond Willey who had been so helpful in getting me a job as clerk in the consulate in Budapest and then had recommended me for his job as Consular Agent in Fiume, now offered me a job with his company, the Harbison-Walker Refractories, of Pittsburgh, manufacturers of fireproof bricks. I was assigned to the company's plant in Portsmouth, Ohio, but I remained there only a few weeks, because I realized that in Portsmouth I would have no opportunity for the kind of schooling I needed.

On my return to New York, I found it hard to get a job. The experience I had gained abroad was of little value in connection with available jobs in the United States. I soon realized that I would have to start at the very bottom of the ladder. I got a temporary job with the Society for the Prevention of Cruelty to Children, translating parts of the French penal code pertaining to children. This paid me $10 a week. Then I got a job with a steamship company at $15 a week. I found that if I learned stenography, I could earn more money. An ad in the newspapers offered

62

a complete course in stenography for $7.50 at the Pratt School. I paid my $7.50 and at the end of six weeks got a job as stenographer with Abercrombie & Fitch, where I received $20 a week, which was considered good pay in those days.

In the meantime I had taken the United States Civil Service examination for interpreter at Ellis Island. Robert Watchhorn was then Commissioner of Immigration in New York. He was most helpful to me. Because I knew Croatian, as well as Italian and German, my name was placed high on the eligible list, and soon Mr. Watchhorn was able to assign me to an interpreter's job at Ellis Island at $1,200 a year. This enabled me to go through law school in night classes relatively free from economic worries.

On applying for entrance to New York University Law School, I learned much to my chagrin that the certificates I had from the Arizona schools were not satisfactory to the Regents of the State of New York. I was therefore required to take Regents' examinations for the equivalent of pre-law school courses, and I had to do some "boning." In one group of examinations I made all the points needed except four and completed those the next term. The New York Preparatory School, which I entered for the purpose of studying for Regents' examinations, poured the stuff into us as fast as any individual could absorb it. My stay in Europe had not been entirely wasted, for besides my knowledge of languages, the general reading I had done in history came in handy.

I entered New York University Law School in 1907, taking my courses in the evening after my full day's work over on Ellis Island. The work on the Island was difficult and strenuous. For two years we worked seven days a week, for immigration was very heavy at this time. All of us were glad, however, to have the jobs, despite the long hours and tiring tasks. Immigrants were pouring in at the average rate of 5,000 a day, and it was a constant grind from the moment we got into our uniforms early in the morning until the last minute before we left on the 5:30 boat in the evening. We had to catch the 8:40 ferry every morning.

2

The immigration laws were rigidly enforced, and there were many heartbreaking scenes on Ellis Island. I never managed during the three years I worked there to become callous to the mental anguish, the disappointment and the despair I witnessed almost daily. Some of the employees did become callous to the suffering after a while, but on the whole they were a hardworking lot, conscientious and loyal. Some of them are still in the Immigration Service.

The importance of inspecting immigrants at the ports of embarkation was brought home to me more forcibly than ever in my everyday experience at Ellis Island. Several hundred immigrants daily were found to be suffering from trachoma, and their exclusion was mandatory. It was harrowing to see families separated because the precaution had not been taken of giving them prior examinations on the other side. Sometimes, if it was a young child who suffered from trachoma, one of the parents had to return to the native country with the rejected member of the family. When they learned their fate, they were stunned. They had never felt ill. They had never heard the word trachoma. They could see all right, and they had no homes to return to. I suffered because I felt so powerless to help these poor people, and I did what I could by writing letters to Senators and Representatives telling them of my experience at Fiume, and urging legislation to remedy the situation. Everyone seemed to agree that the law should require a physical examination at the port of embarkation. But nothing was done about it officially until 1919, when such a law was passed.

The physical requirements for immigrants were very high, and a large percentage were excluded for medical reasons. In addition to trachoma, cases of favus and other scalp diseases were common. I always suffered greatly when I was assigned to interpret for mental cases in the Ellis Island hospital. I felt then, and I feel the same today, that over fifty per cent of the deportations for alleged mental disease were unjustified. Many of those classified as mental cases were so classified because of ignorance on the part of the immigrants or the doctors and the inability of the doctors to understand the particular immigrant's norm, or standard.

One case haunted me for years. A young girl in her teens from the mountains of northern Italy turned up at Ellis Island. No one understood her particular dialect very well, and because of her hesitancy in replying to questions she did not understand, she was sent to the hospital for observation. I could imagine the effect on this girl, who had always been carefully sheltered and had never been permitted to be in the company of a man alone, when a doctor suddenly rapped her on the knees, looked into her eyes, turned her on her back and tickled her spine to ascertain her reflexes. The child rebelled—and how! It was the cruelest case I ever witnessed on the Island. In two weeks' time that child was a raving maniac, although she had been sound and normal when she arrived at Ellis Island.

Under the Immigration Law, contract laborers who have been induced, assisted, encouraged or solicited to migrate to this country by offers or promises of employment are excluded. The application of the contract labor provision of the law during my day in the Immigration Service was anything but uniform. Some of the inspectors were clever about questioning the immigrants and trapping them into admitting that they had offers or promises of jobs.

It is a puzzling fact that one provision of the Immigration Law excludes any immigrant who has no job and classifies him as likely to become a public charge, while another provision excludes an immigrant if he has a job! Common sense suggested that any immigrant who came into the United States in those days to settle here permanently surely came here to work. However, under the law, he could not have any more than a vague hope of a job. In answering the inspectors' questions, immigrants had to be very careful, because if their expectations were too enthusiastic, they might be held as coming in violation of the contract labor provision. Yet, if they were too indefinite, if they knew nobody, had no idea where they were going to get jobs, they might be excluded as likely to become public charges. Most of the inspectors were conscientious and fair. Sometimes, I felt, large batches of those held and deported as violating the contract labor provision were, perhaps, only borderline cases and had no more than the assurance from relatives or former townsmen of jobs on their arrival.

While the application and interpretation of the contract labor law might seem on the surface to be extreme, even illogical, the history of immigrant labor in this country fully justified such a law. Before its enactment in the 'eighties, our country went through a period of exploitation of labor which is one of the most sordid and blackest pictures in our entire history. The railroads and our young industries were built by exploited immigrant labor brought here under contract. They were built with the blood and tears and sweat of underpaid, ignorant immigrants. The padrone system flourished for more than twenty-five years before it was weakened by our immigration laws. For some twenty years thereafter, the padrone system continued to operate in a milder form but in just as cruel and greedy a manner, and with just as disastrous results for the poor ignorant immigrants who were subjected to it. Though we have outlived systematized exploitation of labor, the contract labor provision still serves a useful preventive purpose.

Shipload after shipload of immigrants were brought into this country by contractors, or padrones, who had already made contracts with the railroads and other large corporations for their services. The wages, at best, were disgracefully low. In the eighteen nineties these wages averaged $1.25 to $1.50 a day. The padrone was paid by the corporation. In addition to the low wages he paid the laborers, he took a rake-off from their meager daily earnings. In addition to that, he boarded and fed the immigrants, for which he often made exorbitant charges, deducted, too, from their small pay. Often he had a company store as well, in which he sold them supplies at excessive prices. How they ever managed to save enough to send for their families is a wonder. The twelve-hour day was not unusual, and the seven-day week was common.

The parents of some of our splendid citizens went through a life of hardship and sacrifice. It is no wonder that so many of their children have made valuable contributions to American life, for they valued what they and their parents got after such effort. It annoys me greatly whenever I hear thoughtless people, often raised the easy way, who have never known any of the hardships these immigrant families endured every day, hurl insults at American citizens who have in many cases contributed much more to the welfare of this nation than those who look down upon them or turn their noses up at them. Look around you in any part of this country: the immigrants have contributed more than their share to building its power and its wealth.

Persons convicted of offenses involving moral turpitude .·ere excluded from the country. Immigrants were required to present certificates showing them free from penal offenses. Some did not have them, and others would not present them. That created a presumption of guilt, and then the immigrants were questioned very closely. I discovered that many were being deported for minor offenses or because of incorrect interpretation of their answers or inaccurate translations of their penal certificates. I got the translators together, and we brought about some uniformity in the translation of these crimes, and that prevented a lot of injustice.

There were some rare cases of husbands who had sent for their wives after two or three years of hard working and saving from their small wages, only to learn for the first time that a child had been born in the meantime. We also witnessed scenes of great generosity, understanding and forgiveness.

Often we interpreters at Ellis Island had to accompany couples to the city to be married. These were cases of young men who had sent for their fiancées. The men would arrive at Ellis Island all prepared to marry before admission had been granted to the young ladies. We would take them to the City Hall in New York, where marriages were performed in those days by aldermen. The aldermen took turns performing the ceremonies and getting the fees. Some of the aldermen were not averse to getting a little extra, above the two dollars prescribed by the law. I know that most of the Immigration Service personnel protected the immigrants and were not parties to these overcharges.

I was assigned to only a few of these cases, but a few were plenty. I would escort the bridegroom and his bride and their witnesses to the City Hall to see that they were properly married and then give the bride clearance for admission to the country. In the few instances I attended the aldermen were drunk. Some of the aldermen would insert into their reading of the marriage ceremony remarks they considered funny and sometimes used lewd language, much to the amusement of the red-faced, cheap "tinhorn" politicians who hung around them to watch the so-called fun. I was happy when years later the law granting aldermen authority to perform marriages was repealed. Later, as Mayor, I had occasion to improve conditions in the City Clerk's office, where systematized graft in marriage fees and licenses had been going on, and my early experience with this contemptible petty thievery made me all the more eager to improve those conditions.

On the whole, the personnel of the Immigration Service was kindly and considerate. At best, the work was an ordeal. Our compensation, besides our salaries, for the heartbreaking scenes we witnessed, was the realization that a large percentage of these people pouring into Ellis Island would probably make good and enjoy a better life than they had been accustomed to where they came from.

The time is not distant when our country will be looking around for more immigrants. Within a few years there will be great need for more unskilled workers, domestic help and manual laborers. Perhaps we shall have to work out a system of seasonal immigration for some workers. Before long there will be a shortage of labor in our coal mines, and these immigrants will have to be permanent residents. I hope that we shall learn from our past experience and build staffs of understanding, considerate men and women interpreting a careful, consistent body of immigration law adequate for the new immigration we shall require.

3

During the last year of my three years' service at Ellis Island, I was assigned to the Night Court, as an interpreter. This was very helpful to me, for it permitted me to take my last year's work at law school in the daytime and saved me time going back and forth to Ellis Island.

The Night Court at that time, 1910, dealt exclusively with cases of commercialized vice. The Immigration Service was interested in aliens who were engaged in such practice. I had to interview defendants brought into Night Court and to ascertain from them their place of birth, and, if they were foreign-born, the dates of their arrival. If any of them had been here less than five years, warrants were issued and upon proper proof they were deported. I interviewed an average of thirty to forty such persons every night for a whole year.

Some of these cases were very pathetic. In this work I got a liberal education in the ways of the Police Department, experience that was very helpful to me later on. I venture to state that the suppression of commercialized vice during my administration as Mayor was more efficient than at any previous time. We just did not tolerate police corruption and were determined to wipe it out.

That some of the police were corrupt in 1910 was easy to see. It was not at all unusual for a patrol wagon full of women to draw up to the Night Court. The policemen and the victims would suddenly learn that there had been a substitution of judges. A "jail judge" was sitting instead of a "fining judge." The clamor among the girls was then great. I used to see police officers reluctantly return money to the girls. When a "fining judge" was sitting, more cases were brought into court. The grafters were thus able to maintain their record for arrests and do a thriving business.

I can still see the faces of numerous men who practiced at the bar of this Women's Night Court. To me it was clear that this was a dirty trade. Some of the lawyers were eventually disbarred. But, surprisingly, some made good. They would take cases in those days for anything from two dollars to about twenty-five, which was usually the fee for defending a woman on the charge of "keeping and maintaining" a house of prostitution. Some of these former gentlemen of the Night Court bar in 1910 hold high office today. One whose name I recall has an important judicial post today. It was strange to me then, and it is strange to me today, how these individuals could justify their way of making a living. Though the procedure has been improved since 1910, it is by no means perfect. At least, there is an opportunity today of ascertaining disease and providing for proper cure, which did not exist when I was a young interpreter.

The probation system, too, was in its infancy at that time. Though it was unorganized, it was effective, and there was not so much so-called scientific approach. However, the system was tender and humane. Miss Alice Smith was the probation officer in the Night Court in 1910. She is the mother of probation in New York City. Miss Smith sat in a side room off the court room. In the back of the court room sat the representative of the Florence Crittenton League. Welfare and religious organizations did not go in for that kind of work in those days, and nothing that exists today can take the place of the kindliness, hospitality and understanding of that Florence Crittenton League of those days. It had a little home in Bleecker Street. Young girls who were immature first offenders were turned over to Miss Luther, of the Florence Crittenton Home, at the end of the court session. Miss Luther would toddle off with them. There were no guards, no locked doors in that little house in Bleecker Street. That is why the girls didn't run away. There was always a pot of coffee on the stove. The whole treatment of the girls was so simple, so sweet and so nice.

Miss Smith, the probation officer of Night Court, would get to work to find the girls jobs in the effort to rehabilitate them. No public funds were availabe, but Miss Smith had friends who would always provide the money for a new outfit of clothes, shoes, dental work, or whatever else the girls desperately needed before they could get respectable work. Among the people who supplied Miss Smith with funds for this worthy cause were Jules S. Bache, John D. Rockefeller, Andrew Freedman, and Miss Kelso, who was one of the editors of Street & Smith publications.

The percentage of girls who were salvaged by this simple, humane and original probation work was very high. The hardened cases, the repeaters, would be the first to say to a "kid" in the station house, the patrol wagon or the detention cell at Night Court, "Hey, kid, get out of this while you can. Tell the judge you want to talk to Miss Smith."

From my experience in the Night Court I would say that ninety-five per cent of such cases brought into court then were the results of economic pressure. Provided there is increasing economic security, and provided enforcement agencies keep after the professional procurers who exploit these unfortunate girls, there will be less and less commercialized vice in New York. Of the hundreds and hundreds of cases I interviewed, I do not believe that there were more than four or five above average intellect, or who had more than fifth or sixth grade schooling. The living wage now paid to many unskilled women workers is the greatest factor in reducing the number of these victims of social evil.

The White Slave Division of the Immigration Service was constantly on the alert for persons who imported immigrants for immoral purposes. Such systematized importation was pretty well broken up by the time I entered the service. It had flourished during the eighteen nineties, but with the amendment of the Immigration Law, putting teeth in it and broadening the powers of the Immigration Service on deportation, organized importation of white slaves was rare in 1910, although there were some stray cases.

One of the Assistant United States Attorneys who prosecuted white slave cases, and whom I got to know and remained friendly with thereafter was a young lawyer of ability and sincerity. His name was Felix Frankfurter.

The inspector in charge of the White Slave Division of the Immigration Service was a man named Andrew Tedesco. He knew many languages, was unkempt and unprepossessing in appearance. But to Tedesco belongs most of the credit for preventing importation of white slaves from foreign countries on a systematized basis. He faced the opposition of hotels, resorts and politicians. To all in those trades this white slave traffic was potentially profitable. A lot of them weren't worried about how widespread the traffic became, so long as it went on quietly and did not interfere with the comfort or disturb the feelings of their other patrons who did not know it was going on under the same roof where they were spending their holidays or leading their more respectable lives. Tedesco cleaned up the red light district along Sixth Avenue, which was part of the notorious Tenderloin.

When I was first assigned to Night Court, Tedesco said to me: "You can get experience in this job, or you can make a great deal of money. I don't think you'll take the money. But, remember, the test is if you hesitate. Unless you say 'No!' right off, the first time an offer comes your way, you're gone."

I always remembered that bit of advice throughout my career. It was the first, instinctive reaction to dishonesty or indecency that always counted, and I have repeated Tedesco's advice to many men entering public service where they are subject to temptation.

CHAPTER IV

Law and Politics

1

I PROFITED GREATLY by my studies at New York University Law School. I had plenty of incentive to study law rather than merely to cram for a bar examination as many of my classmates were doing, because my time and resources were so limited. It seemed to me then, as it has ever since, that too many lawyers were being turned out like so many sausages every year. It was obvious that many of the young men in our classes had neither the mental equipment nor the educational background needed to make good lawyers. Yet there they were, being turned out and going into active practice.

I remember three of my fellow students particularly. Two of them I found on the bench later, when I became Mayor, Bill Clapp and Anna Kross. The third had a brilliant mind, but it had a peculiar twist to it. I predicted to some of my friends at NYU that he would land up in jail. He did.

I was much impressed by the splendid corps of instructors at NYU Law School. Anybody who did have the interest, the mental equipment and the educational background had plenty of chance to get a good grounding in the law at that school. I remember particularly that our course in Constitutional law under Isaac Franklin Russell was a liberal education in itself. Professor Russell was a most erudite scholar and had a great store of knowledge. He was better in the evening class than in the afternoon, for between the two he would go to a near-by French or Italian restaurant in Greenwich Village and would be quite mellow for the evening class. I found what he taught me most useful in later years. After my three years of study at NYU, I had no trouble passing the bar examination and was satisfied that I had learned how to use "the tools of the trade."

I started in the law business on the first day I was admitted to the bar in October 1910. I went to Ellis Island that day to see Byron Uhl, Acting Commissioner of Immigration. He had been in the Immigration Service for more than thirty years. He was a strict disciplinarian. I handed him my resignation and asked him if he thought I was doing right. He smiled, stood up, took me by the arm and led me to the door of an adjoining room. He pointed to two of the employees sitting there. Then he took me out on a sort of balcony around the main hall and pointed to three or four of the inspectors. "Fiorello," he said, "they are all lawyers. They are discouraged and unhappy, and they are too old to start practicing now. You are doing the right thing. Best of luck to you."

I had two weeks' salary from my job at Ellis Island, amounting to a total capital of $65. I rented office space at $15 a month in the law offices of McIlheny and Bennett. William M. Bennett, one of the partners, was active in politics as well as the law. He was naturally an insurgent, but he was not a progressive, and his insurgency was limited to fighting the Republican machine. He had managed to get himself elected State Senator in the face of the opposition of the party machine. In 1917, when John Purroy Mitchel was the unanimous choice of the Republican Party for renomination for Mayor, William M. Bennett filed petitions, and without any organization back of him, took the nomination away from Mayor Mitchel. Mitchel ran as an independent, and John F. Hylan was elected Mayor on the regular Democratic ticket.

I was to run into my friend Bill Bennett again on two occasions, after I had entered politics myself. He ran against me in 1919 for the nomination for President of the Board of Aldermen, and I won. In 1929, when I ran for Mayor against Jimmy Walker, a surprising situation developed. I had been seeing quite a bit of Bill Bennett, and he seemed interested in my nomination. He was absolutely sincere in his efforts for good government. We had one thing in common: neither of us liked a political machine. Bennett was giving me good advice for the coming campaign.

I cannot describe my astonishment when one morning I read in an exclusive story in the New York *Times* that Bill Bennett had entered the Republican primaries to contest the nomination with me. The *Times* article contained a long statement by Bennett attacking my candidacy. I just couldn't believe it.

I later learned that Bill Bennett was just as surprised by that article as I was. The whole thing had been cooked up by a writer on the New York *Times*. This man always opposed me for every nomination I received for public office, even when his own paper, editorially at least, was supporting me. The late Adolph Ochs, who was as different from the *Times* administration which took over after his death as day is from night, told me frankly that he had complete confidence in this writer. The man took full advantage of that confidence.

I learned not only from Bill Bennett himself, but from members of his immediate family that he had been trapped into making that statement about my candidacy. Bennett was living at the time in the old Murray Hill Hotel. One evening a bottle of synthetic gin was consumed during the course of a discussion of political events in Bennett's apartment. It was at this session, Bennett and the members of his family told me, that he signed a statement of which he had absolutely no recollection afterwards. Then he read it in the New York *Times* and asked a reporter about it.

Meanwhile, petitions for Bennett's nomination had been obtained. There was quite a racket in petitions for nominations at that time. One group, since put out of business, would obtain signatures and sell them for so much per signature. I didn't have the money to contest the validity of the Bennett petitions, and the Republican organization, which was already working for Jimmy Walker behind the scenes, didn't care to help. I had to work hard to win the nomination in the Republican primary before starting my strenuous campaign against Tammany in 1929. Bill Bennett was ashamed of what had happened.

When I had moved into Bennett's offices at 15 William Street to begin my practice of the law, I managed to get some letterheads and some secondhand furniture. The firm had a good law library, and I had a good legal education. I was hopeful, but I had no particular passion for the practice of the law. My practice, however, was most useful and gave me an opportunity to learn a great deal about conditions in New York courts and New York politics in relation to the courts, which came in handy later when I held office in New York City.

The more I got to know about lawyers and their ethics, the less respect I had for them. I needed business about as badly as any young lawyer in the game, but I look back now and am happy in the knowledge that I never took a case that I did not believe in. I never accepted a retainer unless I was convinced of the rights of my client. I found that nine persons out of ten who consult lawyers have either no need for a lawyer or no case. I refused to take cases when I thought the client had no case or did not need a lawyer but could settle his differences himself. I lost many, many clients who became fine friends of mine in later years. They would seldom believe me when I advised them that they had no case and would run to other lawyers, who would sometimes exaggerate the importance of their cases, talk a lot of legal gibberish to impress them, take a fee, which the client, in time, would have to charge off to experience. It would have been easy to build up a large practice, if I had done the same as they, but I liked it better the other way.

Later, when I went to Congress, I saw how easy it was to exploit public office to get law business. But I thought there was only one thing to do and that was to devote my time to my Congressional duties. Even lawyers tried to retain me to appear in government cases or before government departments. Members of Congress, of course, are forbidden by law to engage in such practice. However, strangely enough, a great deal of it was going on during the seven terms I served in the House of Representatives.

2

Soon after I began to practice law, I got some familiarity with the workings of our courts in New York City. One of the first things that one noted was that knowing the judge did not injure any lawyer. I remember still my first case in the Municipal Court. I prepared it carefully, and the facts were properly presented. The judge decided it against me. I could not figure out why. The judge called me up to the bench. He knew I was a young lawyer recently admitted to the bar. He congratulated me on my presentation of the case. "Well, if I did so well, why didn't you decide in my favor?" I asked. "Oh, young man, I'll give you a break some other day," he said. What a hell of a way to dispense justice! I thought. This same judge is now on the bench of the New York Supreme Court.

I did not go in for criminal cases, and I don't suppose I ever had more than ten or twelve such cases to try. I do not remember ever having taken a fee for a criminal case. Most of those I tried were either assigned to me by the court or cases I accepted because friends or settlement house workers solicited my interest when the families involved had no money to retain a lawyer.

Some of the few criminal cases I had were pretty tough. I remember falling right into a particularly bad one. One day I was in the court room just before the luncheon recess, waiting to keep an appointment with Judge Morris Koenig. Before he became a judge he was very helpful in my first successful campaign for Congress in 1916.

There was quite a stir in the court that day. Some defendants were brought up for pleading, among them a small man. I was paying no particular attention to the procedure, when, suddenly, the judge said to me, "Congressman, do you speak French?" Always willing to show off, I said, "Yes, Your Honor." As a matter of fact, my French could be classified as anything but "speaking French." Then the judge said, "I appoint Congressman La Guardia as defense counsel."

Even then I thought it was just a matter of pleading. I stepped up to the bar and there met my client, who had just been extradited from France. He was one of four defendants who had committed one of the cruelest crimes ever perpetrated in the city. Three of his accomplices had already been convicted and were serving long sentences in Sing Sing.

I asked my client, Paul Camillieri, alias "The Jockey" and "Petit François," because he was so small, "Do you wish to plead guilty or not guilty?" "I am innocent," he answered. "How can I plead guilty?" Whereupon, I pleaded him not guilty and thought my job was ended. At lunch I asked Judge Koenig whether I had to continue, and he said, "Absolutely. This man is facing a fifty-year jail sentence. The county has spent a great deal of money locating him and bringing him back from France. His associates are now serving sentences of twenty-five to forty years." I was in for it all right. I had to defend a mean, cruel little crook, who was as stubborn a client as any lawyer ever had to handle.

The case concerned the Shattuck family, who lived at 19 Washington Square North. Albert R. Shattuck was a retired banker in his late sixties. His wife was the daughter of William L. Strong, reform Mayor of New York from 1895 until 1897. They were people of wealth, culture and refinement. They maintained quite an establishment in

Washington Square, with eight servants. Among these was a Corsican butler, Alphonse Gabriel Mourey. He planned the robbery of his employers and enlisted the aid of accomplices, including my client, who had a long criminal record in France.

On Sunday, April 2, 1922, the Corsican butler Mourey arranged for his four accomplices to enter the Shattuck mansion through a manhole and coal shuttle while his employers were in church. When they returned, three masked men entered Mrs. Shattuck's room, seized her, pressed pistols to her temple, heart and side and demanded in French, "Money and diamonds." Meanwhile, the other two robbers were covering the servants in the kitchen. My client, Paul Camillieri, and a companion searched Mrs. Shattuck's room, while the third robber guarded her. They threatened to torture her if she made any noise. Rings were torn from her fingers, and finally she was dragged downstairs and herded with Mr. Shattuck and the servants into the wine cellar, which had a sort of refrigerator-safe door. Before she was pushed into the cellar, Mrs. Shattuck asked permission to pray. Camillieri shouted at her: "Do not ask God to prolong your life, but ask Him to forgive your sins." Then he slammed the wine cellar door on her and the rest of the household. This gave the robbers plenty of time to select all the jewelry and other valuables they wanted and to try to make a getaway.

Meanwhile, working with a small penknife and a dime, Mr. Shattuck loosened the screws and lock of the refrigerator door. It took him a long time, and some of the servants were about to lose consciousness when he finally succeeded in opening the door. The robbers, who were still ransacking the house, had expected the people in the cellar to be asphyxiated. They fled down the street. Mrs. Shattuck ran after them with two pistols she had picked up from the floor. One of the men, Eugene Diaset, was caught a few blocks away and another, Morse Bagnoli, was captured by the police soon after the crime. The others, including my client, escaped to France.

Diaset and Bagnoli were tried on April 21, 1922, pleaded guilty to burglary in the first degree, and gave the names of their associates. Judge Rosalsky sentenced them to State prison for not less than forty and not more than sixty years. Mr. Shattuck offered rewards for the capture of the others, and he had posters printed in twelve languages, offering these rewards, sending them to police stations in every major country of five continents. He made two trips to Europe in the effort to track them down. Arrests of suspects were made throughout the world, some being picked up in Port Said, Irkutsk, Paris, Berlin, London and New York.

The butler, Mourey, got to France and avoided capture until he was finally surrounded by gendarmes near Paris and fought a pistol battle with them in which he was seriously wounded. He was tried and sentenced to be guillotined. Mr. Shattuck requested commutation of Mourey's sentence to life imprisonment, which was done, and Shattuck rewarded the Paris police with $15,000.

My client, Paul Camillieri, was finally caught in France, escaped and was recaptured. He went on a hunger strike. Brought here on the *Leviathan* by two New York detectives, "The Jockey," then thirty-four, nervous and stunted, tried to cut his throat while he was being shaved in the ship's barber shop. He had almost chewed off the ends of his fingers to prevent identification, and he had to be chained in his stateroom and watched day and night.

Camillieri was arraigned before Judge Morris Koenig on July 22, 1924, the day when, unluckily, I happened to be waiting in court for the judge. He was held without bail on two indictments charging robbery and one charging burglary. He insisted the charges were a frame-up by the Paris police to get him out of France, and that he had never been in this country before being brought here by the New York detectives.

I received a court order to have witnesses in France examined, including the butler, Mourey. The case finally came to trial on May 19, 1925, before Judge Otto Rosalsky, an able jurist and a fair judge, who was very stern with hard criminals, and properly so. Before he went to trial, and even during the trial, I advised "Petit François" to plead guilty. He kept on refusing to do that. I sought to be relieved from the case before it came to trial, and even during the trial, but the judge insisted that it was my duty as an officer of the court to stand by and see to it that the defendant's rights were protected and to use every proper legal means to assert those rights.

The prosecuting attorney was Owen Bohan, who later became a judge of that same Court of General Sessions. The case lasted five or six days. Camillieri's colleagues were brought down from prison and testified against him. They were very bitter toward him, and it was rumored that he had got away with most of the loot and that the others had expected to join him in France. The identification was positive. The jury brought in a verdict of guilty on June 5, 1925, and Judge Rosalsky sentenced my client to not less than forty-five years and not more than sixty-five years.

This hardened criminal could not even behave in jail; he was one of the leaders of a group who staged a jailbreak some years later. I suppose he is still in one of our State prisons.

I did not enjoy that trial one bit. Not until it was all over did the jury know that I had been assigned to the case. The judge was good enough to tell them that after their verdict and to thank me for my service to the State. I never boasted about my French again.

3

The personality of the judge has the greatest effect on the course of justice, and on the fate of the men brought before them. I had one experience which demonstrated that fact. I was trying a case before Judge Joseph F. Mulqueen in the Court of General Sessions.

A perfectly no-good loafer who wouldn't work had got into trouble in a crooked card game. His wife was a fine, hardworking woman. She had a good job and kept the family going. She appealed to me to defend her husband, who was charged with robbery. It was another of those cases where there was no money available for a lawyer. The neighbors had said, "Go to La Guardia."

When I looked into the case, I found that it was a typical instance where the police wanted to make a "build-up" to show that they were coping with the particularly bad conditions on the lower West Side at that time. There was no doubt in my mind that the card game in which my client had been involved with some sailors was not on the level. The fellow was guilty of taking part in a crooked card game, but from the witnesses I interviewed, I learned that the sailors had left the place long before he had, and that he could prove that he had gone directly home and therefore could not be guilty of robbing them. I had heard a great deal about frame-ups, and here was one that was perfect. In all frame-ups the evidence is usually pretty compact.

Judge Mulqueen, even when he was feeling good, was quite temperamental. That particular day in court he was feeling anything but good. Lawyers hated to try cases before him, and witnesses and jurymen were frightened by his irascibility. I was young and not at all experienced in the customs and atmosphere of the Court of General Sessions. I started to defend my client in a lawyer-like way. Early in the trial came my first clash with the judge, and clashes continued throughout the proceedings. The old lawyers who frequented that court and some top lawyers who were waiting for their cases to be called came up to me at recess time, patted me on the back, praised my work and urged me on. I was fool enough to fall for it. They were having a good time at my expense and egging me on to do what none of them dared to do, combat the judge's temperament.

In my summation I told the jury to pay no attention to the judge's attitude. It was apparent, I said, that the judge was trying the case instead of the District Attorney. Anyone could see how prejudiced he was, I stated, and pointed out that under the law it was for the jury to decide the facts on the evidence, and that the evidence showed that my client had not committed a robbery.

Judge Mulqueen's charge to the jury was a stinger. He

went out of his way to make disparaging remarks about "fresh young lawyers." The jury retired. As soon as the jury had left the room, Judge Mulqueen said in open court: "Young man, if the jury finds your client guilty, I am going to give him twenty years, and he can thank you for it. Let this be a lesson to you." Naturally, I remonstrated. I told the judge not to take out his resentment against me on my client; if I had done anything wrong, he could punish me, but I had defended my client to the best of my ability, as it was my duty to do.

The jury brought in a verdict of guilty, and Judge Mulqueen then and there sentenced my client to twenty years—straight. I felt very bad about that, of course. The judge also gave me another fierce bawling-out. The family felt that the sentence was my fault. The neighbors got together and took up a collection for an appeal, but the case was lost in the higher court. I never forgot that experience, and I never tried a case before Judge Mulqueen again.

Three or four years later, I returned from overseas after participating in World War I. I was then living at the Hotel Brevoort. One evening Judge Rosalsky telephoned me and asked if he could come down to see me. He told me this story: Judge Mulqueen was frantic with worry. The war was over, and he had not heard a word from his son in more than three months. He had tried to get information from every possible source. His son's outfit had returned home, but the son was not with them. Nobody seemed to know his whereabouts. Judge Rosalsky had said to Mulqueen: "Let's ask Congressman La Guardia to help. He was in the Army and is very active in military matters. Perhaps he can find out." "Oh no, don't ask him," Judge Mulqueen had replied, but Judge Rosalsky came to me anyway.

I sent a telegram to General Pershing giving the facts. The boy was located. He had had a severe case of influenza and had been shifted from his outfit to a hospital. In the confusion of demobilization his papers were lost. In three days I got a telegram from GHQ, Chaumont, informing me that the boy was convalescing. I immediately telephoned the information to Judge Rosalsky.

A few days later I was lunching in downtown New York. I don't know whether by design or accident, but Judge Rosalsky walked in with Judge Mulqueen. Judge Mulqueen walked over to my table and thanked me with the sincerity and emotion of a father. He was human at that moment. As he was starting to leave, he turned around and said: "Congressman, I remember a case you tried before me. I have been thinking about it. I think I was a little harsh. I am going to see what I can do about it." Judge Mulqueen, on his own initiative, wrote to the Governor and got a commutation of sentence for my client. There was a streak of kindness in the old grouch.

The personality of the judge had an effect in some of the interesting civil cases I tried. Because of the personal traits of judges one could never be sure that a case would be decided on its merits. I remember one case of breach of warranty in which there was a perfectly good defense because the goods sold and delivered by a wholesale grocery firm were defective, and the vendor had refused to accept return of the merchandise, which were a total loss to the purchaser. At the end of the trial, however, the judge said to the jury: "Now, gentlemen, if you want to retire, you may, but I don't think it is necessary. There is a very clear case of goods sold and delivered and not paid for." But the jury did want to retire. The judge expressed surprise. It was late in the afternoon. Two or three times I noticed the court attendant come up and talk to the judge. The lawyer for the plaintiff was a former partner of this judge. Finally, the jury brought in a verdict for the plaintiff. I learned a few years later from one of the jurymen, whom I happened to meet, that the judge had sent word to the jury to hurry up with the decision and come in with a verdict for the plaintiff.

In another case I was trying for a woman who was injured through the gross negligence of a motorman on a Brooklyn trolley car, the judge was pretty rough to our side all the way through. The jury went out. I was in the hallway. The judge, on his way from the court room to his chambers, accosted the lawyer for the trolley line. "Was it all right, Joe?" he asked. Perhaps he didn't see me, but he ignored me if he did and did not care whether I heard him or not. Then he added to his friend the traction lawyer: "Well, Joe, don't worry. If they bring in a verdict against you, I will set it aside."

Later I studied the system by which judges were selected for nomination and found that most of them were hand-picked by politicians. The bar association would go through the motions of endorsing or refusing to endorse candidates. I learned that any judge who had a chance of election was pretty sure to get the endorsement of the bar associations. When I was Mayor, I consulted the bar associations on one of my first judicial appointments. I found that three out of five of the members of the bar association committee on appointments were candidates themselves for this judgeship! I thought maybe that was just a coincidence. But I did not get much help from the bar associations during my years as Mayor. I also discovered when I looked into the situation on selection of judges that any judge who had served a term, no matter how bad he might be, had ninety-nine chances out of a hundred of getting an endorsement for renomination by the bar associations. I hate to say that. I have so many good friends who are prominent in the bar associations of New York City, and who are fine, upstanding men, a credit to their profession. Yet the fact remains that the calibre of the judges in this State, on the whole, through the years, bears out what I say. Oh, yes, there are some excellent judges, scholarly, upright, hardworking, fair. They are the exceptions. Later, when I was a Congressman, I brought impeachment proceedings against several federal judges. Some of those men in our high federal courts were neither upright nor scholarly, and some of them bore no resemblance to Caesar's wife.

I often sought in later times to have a "Who's Who" of judges' secretaries drawn up and published. It would have been a shock to most citizens. My idea was never taken up. Some of the secretaries of judges, drawing around $10,000 a year in salaries, know no law. Most of them know the district leaders. Some of them have very little education of any kind. Some even had criminal records themselves. They are selected for their politics and their friendships, and this is one of the most pernicious results of the patronage system. Some day this entire method of selection of judges, determination of their qualifications and those of their assistants in New York State will have to be changed, if we are to attain an approach to decent justice.

4

During the period when I began to practice law in New York, that city had become the greatest garment manufacturing center in the country. Many fortunes were made in this business. And they were made out of exploitation of labor. Ninety-five per cent of the needle trades workers on dresses, cloaks and suits were newly arrived immigrants. They had to take whatever wages and working conditions were offered to them. They were crowded into dark, unsanitary workshops, worked ten to twelve hours a day, a 72- to 80- hour week, at shamefully low wages. The work was seasonal. For some fifteen to twenty weeks a year these people were unemployed. They lived in overcrowded, disease-infested old-law tenements that had been condemned years before but were still in existence.

I had the chance thirty years later when I became Mayor to condemn, vacate and demolish some 160 of these very same shameful dwelling units. Tuberculosis was particularly prevalent among these underpaid, underfed, badly housed garment workers. Yet, many of them survived and raised splendid families. Some gave their lives that their children might have a better existence than they themselves had ever known.

All that is past. Wages in the clothing industries now amount to a decent annual income. All of the workers live properly and decently. Tuberculosis has virtually disappeared among them. Factory laws prevent a return to sweatshop conditions. But these gains were not made without a desperate struggle on the part of the unions and their workers, and it took ten to fifteen years to change those conditions. I was happy to have the chance to participate in some of the clothing workers' early battles for a better life.

The effort of the unions to organize the garment workers was accomplished with the greatest difficulty and only after some big and costly strikes. The increasing greed of the employers made it possible for the unions to get a start, but in the beginning their work had to be kept quite secret.

The strike of the waist and dress makers in New York in the fall of 1909 was the largest strike of women in the United States up to that time. It resulted in many more workers joining the International Ladies' Garment Workers' Union. This pioneer strike is known as the "Uprising of the Twenty Thousand" in labor history, for that many women and girls were out before it was over. When the strike started, Ladies' Waist Makers' Union, Local 25, the main union in that trade then, had about 100 members and $4 in its treasury. The strike began in the shops of the Leiserson Company and the Triangle Waist Company. The manufacturers hired thugs to beat up strikers and prostitutes to fight off pickets. The police worked for the manufacturers and beat up pickets, carrying them off to jail for peacefully picketing.

Members of the Women's Trade Union League joined the picket line and thus brought the cause of these girls to the public's attention. Mass meetings were held to plead the cause of the strikers and to raise money for them. Sam Gompers, Meyer London, Socialist leader, Jacob Panken, labor lawyer, Rabbi Wise and Martin W. Littleton, prominent lawyer, spoke on behalf of the strikers, and there were many protests against the action of the police against pickets.

Magistrate Olmstead, sentencing a girl striker to the workhouse, said to her: "You are on strike against God and Nature, whose law is that man shall earn his bread in the sweat of his brow. You are on strike against God." The Women's Trade Union League cabled this statement to George Bernard Shaw for his comment. "Delightful," he replied. "Medieval America always in the intimate personal confidence of the Almighty."

Dozens of young girls were dragged to police stations every day and fined or sent to the workhouse by magistrates. From the time the strike began in September 1909 until Christmas Day, 723 women were arrested and 19 of them sentenced to the workhouse.

Concerning one of the mass meetings for the strikers the New York *Times* reported that "socialism, unionism, woman suffrage, and what seemed to be something like anarchism were poured into the ears of fully 8,000 persons who gathered." Anne Morgan, Elisabeth Marbury and Mrs. O. H. P. Belmont arranged a meeting at the Colony Club, leading society women's club of New York, where John Mitchell, head of the United Mine Workers, and Rose Schneiderman, labor leader, told the women about the case of the strikers. At this meeting $1,300 was collected for them.

Finally, at the end of December, Marcus M. Marks and John Mitchell succeeded in getting the employers to agree to better conditions, but did not succeed in winning recognition of the union. The workers got a 52-hour week; the employers agreed not to discriminate against those who belonged to a union, and to reinstate the strikers. The strike was said to have cost the workers $100,000, a sum which was then considered "fabulous." But this great strike made the public realize that women workers could engage in successful common endeavor for their industrial welfare, and the foundation was laid for wider union organization and more successful union activity. Local 25, which had about 100 members in September 1909, had 10,000 during the first year after the strike. Other branches of the garment trades workers were inspired by this strike to form unions.

I was studying law and working at Ellis Island and in the Night Court when this big strike was going on and did not take any direct part in it. But I followed its progress and was particularly interested in the picketing problem in New York City. During that period, the right to picket depended on who was doing the picketing, and who was being picketed. Politicians turned picketing into a racket. Unless Tammany lawyers were retained, pickets were jailed. Some of these Tammany lawyers later occupied high judicial and political offices. They were known to the unions as "political lawyers," and their fees were always large. The bondsmen were selected by these "political lawyers." I watched them operate with my own eyes. The unions soon learned that it was prudent, to say the least, to retain the right political lawyers and bondsmen.

Strong-arm men, first employed by the manufacturers, were later used by unions in self-defense to fight the manufacturers' gangsters. This often resulted in real battles which were costly to both sides. It was Sidney Hillman who stepped into this situation and cleaned the gangsters out of his own organization, the Amalgamated Clothing Workers of America. In later strikes the workers were at a disadvantage because all the gangsters were on the manufacturers' side. At the request of Sidney Hillman, I once protested to Mayor Walker about the use of these strong-arm men against the workers and about the protection they were getting from the police. On another occasion I saw Joe Corrigan, then a judge of the Court of General Sessions, about these conditions during a strike. He was an honest and a courageous man. He told me frankly that he would look into the matter, but that if Jimmy Hines, Tammany leader, was back of it, he would be helpless because he could do nothing to men in the Police Department or any other city department if Jimmy Hines had any interest in the affair. Judging from the results of that particular strike, Jimmy Hines must have had some interest in it.

In 1913 the men's clothing workers went on strike. That was a strike involving 65,000 men. They had been working sixty hours a week. Their pay varied from $5 to $14.50 a week. Some skilled workers got $15 and $18 a week. The employers had skillfully pitted Italian workers against Jewish workers and vice versa. The union needed a lawyer to fight picket cases and someone who knew Italian to explain conditions to Italian clothing workers. August Bellanca, head of the Italian section of the Amalgamated, was referred to me. I agreed to help in both phases of this work.

I talked at meetings of Italian workers, persuading them that they had a chance to improve working and living conditions if they would work together. These meetings were my first public appearances and won me many friends and supporters in both Italian and Jewish laboring circles. I found the workers responsive to my appeals in their own languages. Our big job was to get the workers together to work for their common interests.

A splendid group of intelligent young men and women

came out of this important strike of 1913. They sacrificed everything to help improve this exploited mass of immigrant labor. Night after night I spent my time with the union leaders at Local 63, Joint Board, Executive Committee, helping to organize their efforts. During the day I appeared in court to fight cases against pickets and other cases on behalf of the union. The average lawyer at that time shied away from all such cases for fear of incurring unpopularity among the powerful.

I addressed literally hundreds of meetings at that time, and I enjoyed the work immensely, for it gave me a greater sense of accomplishment than routine court work, which might be more remunerative but was less important. I went on the picket line myself outside one of the plants of the Franklyn System on East 32nd Street near First Avenue. I defied the police to arrest me, as they were doing with others, but they refused to touch me and just went on daily interfering with the right of the workers to engage in peaceful picketing.

After the strike had been going on for about two months, we read in the newspapers one Monday morning that it had been settled. No terms had been submitted to the workers, and at union headquarters we did not know the terms of the alleged settlement. Meetings were held all over the city that day. Every available hall was hired. The price of a hall varied from $5 to $15 for a one- or two-hour meeting. We had no union treasury, and the money for the meetings would be picked up in nickels and dimes contributed by the strikers themselves. I never saw such a splendid piece of instantaneous organization. Each meeting selected a delegate. The delegates met and picked a committee. This committee of about fifteen men met around noon in Stuyvesant Hall on Second Avenue and was in session until four o'clock next morning. The committee selected three arbitrators to negotiate with the employers. One of these arbitrators was Meyer London, Socialist leader, who later became a Socialist Congressman from New York and won the respect of his colleagues in the House, though in 1913 he was ostracized and condemned in polite society. Another of the arbitrators was the labor lawyer Jacob Panken, whom I later appointed a judge of the Domestic Relations Court when I became Mayor. I was the third arbitrator.

We had discovered that the United Garment Workers', the A.F. of L. union in the clothing field, had arbitrarily settled the strike without consulting its members or the other strikers who did not belong to that union. Mayor Gaynor ordered the police to stop further picketing on the grounds that the strike was over. The workers issued a statement declaring that they would not return to work under the fake settlement made by the United Garment Workers' leaders.

We three negotiators had a hard time making contact with the employers. They had a committee, but their organization was loose, and they had nothing but contempt for the workers and their representatives. After two days, however, the employers realized that their shops were not going to operate. Then they expressed willingness to sit down with us and talk terms. At first they insisted that the representatives of the United Garment Workers' sit with us, but this we refused. Finally, we managed to work out a settlement for a 53-hour week, which was to become a 52-hour week on the following January first. We also obtained pay increases. After we had reported back to the strikers, in democratic fashion, they consented to return to work.

A few months later these same workers sent delegates to a convention in Nashville, Tennessee, and the Amalgamated Clothing Workers of America was born. Sidney Hillman was chosen its first president. He retained that office until the day of his death in 1946. Hillman was a great organizer and a fine American. He never was a politician, although he got more publicity in the Presidential campaign of 1944 than anybody except the two candidates, because the opposition to President Roosevelt attempted to smear him with communism, and tried to win votes by anti-Semitism. Hillman hated crooked politicians, for he despised dishonesty wherever he met it. It was because of his organizing genius that these underpaid, exploited immigrants formed a model labor organization, and his death was a great loss to the American labor movement.

The A.F. of L regarded the new Amalgamated Clothing Workers in 1913 as an outlaw, and the new union went through some difficult years, fighting twin battles for better conditions and against the old guard in the United Garment Workers'. But the Amalgamated made steady and great advances in improvement of the condition of its workers every year. It finally was taken into the A.F. of L. and remained there until Hillman and some other labor leaders organized the CIO.

The Amalgamated is now one of the outstanding labor organizations in the world. It is honestly, efficiently administered, free from racketeering. Its workers get high wages and working conditions which are as good as in any trade in the country. The union owns and operates a bank in New York and another in Chicago, with resources of about $80,000,000. Both of these banks went through the financial crisis of 1929 without any trouble or without a penny of loss to depositors. They were the first two banks to open after the Bank Holiday of 1933. The Amalgamated naturally took pride in that fact, but some other bankers tried to explain it away by saying that it was an alphabetical accident since Amalgamated began with A.

In addition to its banks the Amalgamated operates two insurance companies, one in New York and the other in Chicago, and has sponsored two housing developments for workers, one on the East Side of New York and the other in the Bronx, which house approximately 1,000 families and cost around $10,000,000; and the union is planning additional housing projects. I have always been proud of my long association with this great organization of workers who changed a big New York industry from sweatshop conditions to almost ideal conditions.

My other work with unions during those years when I was practicing law included negotiations on behalf of the glass workers, who had gone out on strike, and we obtained a much-deserved wage increase for them. I also helped to bring about a settlement in the shirt waist and dress makers' strike of 1916 and was identified with the organization of longshoremen in New York.

5

I practiced law actively from 1910 to 1915 and sporadically in later years when my political activity permitted. I did not accumulate much money, but I managed to live, found time for study and research and certainly learned a great deal about the political and economic conditions in my city.

On several occasions I was offered appointments to the magistrates' bench in New York, which I refused. I was also offered nominations for the higher courts and turned those down. An independent group once offered me the nomination for justice of the Supreme Court of the State of New York. That independent nomination together with the regular party nomination would have meant certain election. By that time I had served two terms in Congress and had been President of the Board of Aldermen in New York. But I had no ambition to be a Supreme Court justice, and I declined. William Randolph Hearst, who was keeping alive his Independence League, by use of which he had sought several times to be Mayor of New York and Governor of the State, asked me to come to see him during the nineteen twenties about my nomination for justice of the Supreme Court. I told him that I was not interested in becoming a judge and wanted to return to Congress. I wanted to make law and not merely to construe it. Also, I did not have the high regard for the courts of our State that a lawyer with judicial ambitions ought to have. Mr. Hearst told me that in all his thirty years' experience in politics up to that time, it was the first instance he had ever encountered of anyone refusing the nomination for Supreme Court justice. He could hardly believe that I meant what I said.

As I have already stated, I joined the Republican Party because I could not stomach Tammany Hall. Again, let it be understood, that when I say Tammany Hall I mean the Democratic political machine in all five boroughs of Greater New York. They are all alike.

I lived in a district in Greenwich Village where the Republican organization was exceptionally clean. It produced suce fine men as Herbert Parsons, Fred Tanner, Henry H. Curran and Frank Stoddard. However, we were a regular political club. History will bear me out when I say that the minority party in any large city can afford to be somewhat virtuous. However, if it happens to get control of the city government, it will resort to the very same activities and indulge in the same bad habits as its rival, assuming it can control the elective officials.

I had been storing up knowledge, and I was eager to bring about better conditions, particularly a more equitable economic situation and less favoritism to special interests in the administration of the law. That was why I was determined to become a Congressman. From the time that I returned to New York after my experience abroad in the Consular Service, I read the *Congressional Record* and kept abreast of activities in Congress. I also made myself familiar with the legislative history of that period. Somehow—I did not know how—I had a feeling that some day I would get into Congress. I kept my eyes open, but I felt that my chances in New York City were very slight. The Republican districts had their Congressmen, but it required a great deal more political influence than I had to obtain a nomination in one of those districts, where nomination meant almost certain election. It was hard to break down the Democratic majorities in their districts. For a time I thought I might go West to a younger state, where the chances were better.

One night I happened to be in the club rooms of the 25th Assembly District, my own district, where I was an election district captain for a time, when the boys were filling in petitions for the nomination for Congress. It was in the late summer of 1914. The petitions were printed, and the names of State and county candidates appeared on them. There were blanks left for the local candidates for the State Senate and Assembly and for representatives in Congress.

Someone hollered out, "Who is the candidate for Congress?" The leader of the district—I think it was Clarence Fay—came from his backroom office. He shouted out, "Who wants to run for Congress?" That was my chance. "I do," I said. "OK, put La Guardia down," Clarence said. That was all there was to it. But I darn near missed out even so. One of the men asked, "Hey, La Guardia, what's your first name?" I said, "Fiorello." "Oh, hell," he said, "let's get someone whose name we can spell." I spelled the name carefully and slowly and had to argue hard to get it on the petitions.

I took my nomination seriously. I soon learned that I was not supposed to take it seriously. When September came along, I attended my first political meeting. It was in one of the district club houses. Pamphlets were distributed throughout the district announcing the meeting, and stating that all the prominent candidates would talk. I was there bright and early. The meeting started. Candidate after candidate spoke. The State candidates came in, and they had the right of way. I waited and waited for my turn. Two or three times in the course of the evening I was sure that I was next when the chairman would say, "And now we will hear from a young and promising candidate." I would get up each time, only to see that someone else was being introduced. The meeting ended around 11:30 that night. I had not been called on. I protested to the chairman, who was talking to the district leader. "How come?" I asked. Everybody had a good laugh. "Why, Fiorello, you haven't a chance of winning," they told me. "We've never elected a Republican to Congress from this district. Now, what you should do is go out and campaign for the State Senator and Assemblyman, help elect the ticket. That is all you can do." "Could I try?" I pleaded. "Oh, no, don't be foolish. You just go out now and help the others, and some day you may get a nomination for an office you can win."

I didn't think that was quite on the level. A few of the boys in the district agreed with me, among them Harry Andrews, who was district secretary, Louis Espresso and old Mike Kehoe. Kehoe, who was in his late seventies, was a master mind and a good political strategist. He was very much amused at my predicament. "Kid, don't be discouraged," he said, "but go out and try."

I discovered that the procedure at that first meeting was repeated at all the regular party meetings. I was not to get a chance to speak at any of them. I went out and bought a secondhand Ford. Harry Andrews and I plastered it with signs, and I started out on my own private, individual campaign. We went from corner to corner every night in that district, and we never missed a wedding, a funeral, a christening or any other kind of a gathering we could get into.

The 14th Congressional District ran from the Hudson River clear across Manhattan to the East River. It included some of the tenement sections of the lower East Side, teeming with Italian and Jewish immigrants. My knowledge of Italian and Yiddish came in handy. I rang doorbells and talked to the immigrant families. At outdoor meetings I would wait until the regular political rally had ended, pull up in my Ford as the people were leaving, gather a crowd and do my talking.

My opponent was Congressman Michael Farley, a saloon-keeper and president of the National Liquor Dealers' Association. He had been the regular Tammany representative in Congress from that district for some time. I was called down once or twice for being "too rough" on him. Distinguished and serious gentlemen in the community pointed out to me that the retail liquor business was a lawful occupation and urged me not to disparage the Congressman who was in that business. I did not disparage him. I merely pointed out that he was not a good Congressman and wasn't even a good bartender.

When the votes were counted that November 1914, Congressman Farley was re-elected by the small margin of 1,700 votes. Never before had the Democratic majority in that district been less than 16,000 votes. Both my Republican colleagues and my Democratic opponents began to take notice of me. The Republicans began to think that maybe I had a future in politics because I could put on a campaign that got the public interested and therefore it would be wise to keep me in the political family. The showing I made attracted enough attention among the politicians to make them think it worth while to give me the appointment of Deputy Attorney General of the State of New York.

The Republicans that year had elected Charles S. Whitman Governor and carried the State, as they usually did in those days, permitting Tammany the rich plunder in the city, by tacit agreement between the bosses of both parties.

CHAPTER V

Public Office and Practical Politics

1

I WAS GLAD to accept the appointment as Deputy Attorney General of the State of New York because of the opportunity to get some experience in public office in my home State. Though I knew that I would gain considerable experience in the law and the way it was administered in New York, I did not know that I was also to learn a great deal about practical politics in that connection. While, of course, I already knew generally that political parties help their friends, I never realized until this experience in the Attorney General's office how far-reaching special privileges and favors really went.

I was assigned to the New York City Bureau of the Attorney General's office in January 1915. The main office, of course, was in Albany. I was given charge of matters ranging from legal work for the State Department of Agriculture to looking into unpaid mortgage taxes and conducting litigation with the federal government. I took my work seriously, though I soon found that not all of the deputies did so and did not seem to be expected to put in a full day's work.

One of the big cases given to me was the matter of the New Jersey fume nuisance. Several factories on the Jersey shore of the Hudson River and one across from Staten Island emanated unpleasant fumes, which caused a great deal of discomfort to the residents of New York, particularly on Washington Heights, Riverside Drive and part of Staten Island. The nuisance had been going on for some years. The official papers relating to this matter filled at least six full file cabinets and a couple of trunks. There were all sorts of chemical and other technical studies and investigations. There was no question about the source of the nuisance nor about its deleterious effects, besides the discomfort and unpleasantness of it.

Several studies of the law in question had been made. Many briefs had been prepared. A Riverside Drive association had spent a great deal of time and money seeking relief from this nuisance. One prominent member of this association, who acted as its attorney, was Charles Craig, who later became Comptroller of the City of New York. As Comptroller his chief delight in life was to make life miserable for Mayor John F. Hylan. When, as President of the Board of Aldermen, I would go to the defense of the Mayor when I thought he was right, I had to absorb a great deal of abuse from Mr. Craig. But in this fume nuisance matter he had done excellent work in preparation of the law to abate the nuisance and in all the legal work for the association interested in accomplishing such abatement.

I was given the case, told to take charge of it and "do something." There were three or four lawyers in the office, senior to me, but I was so excited about getting a case of such importance that I never stopped to consider just why it was given to me. I devoted a great deal of time, day and night, to studying the case and familiarizing myself with all that had happened up to date. It seemed that the Supreme Court of the United States had already pretty well established the law in cases of this kind in its decision in the Tennessee Coal and Iron Company case. I got in touch with the Tennessee officials who had charge of that case and within a few months I had saturated myself with all of the facts and the law.

On two or three former occasions it had been decided by the previous Attorneys General that the State of New York had a right of action and could proceed to abate the nuisance by bringing an action direct in the Supreme Court of the United States, which had original jurisdiction in such cases.

I proceeded to prepare the complaint. There was no secret about it. I got the approval of the chief of our New York Bureau, who, I am quite sure, had the approval of the Attorney General to proceed. So one day I went down to Washington and filed seven complaints in the name of the State of New York against the seven corporations located in New Jersey which we charged with maintaining the nuisance. The fact that the State of New York was filing seven cases at one time against seven large corporations attracted attention, and there was some publicity. I was quite proud of having finally started the actions which had been kicked around the office for at least five or six years. Imagine my surprise when I got a good calling down for proceeding so precipitately. Yes, I had conferred with my chief, but, after all, in a matter of such importance, just getting general acquiescence was not enough, I was told. It was true that the complaint was verified all right and the Attorney General's name was on the complaint. But I had actually taken action in the Supreme Court!

At first I was at a loss to account for this sudden change

of attitude in our office. Well, I soon learned the reason for it. The kick came from Governor Whitman. The party big shots were closely connected with the matter. These corporations had used their tremendous influence, and I was given orders to take no action from now on unless I got direct approval from the chief of the bureau, who, in turn, had to get direct approval from the Attorney General.

The public clamor for relief from the smells continued, and the nuisance continued. It was established that the nuisance could be abated, but it would require quite a considerable expenditure to provide changes in methods of production and equipment. The case dragged on and on. I went to Congress and then to war. When next I inquired about my pet case, I learned that most of the companies involved had made a great deal of money during the war, and that there had been some sort of stipulation that the case would not be pursued but the companies given a liberal amount of time to make the necessary changes. Finally, the fumes ceased by gracious consent of the companies, but so far as the people who suffered from them were concerned, it was the hard way, and no one was fined or otherwise punished for maintaining a nuisance.

Another interesting experience in the Attorney General's office gave me even more knowledge of the ways of politics and justice. It had to do with what might be considered trivial violations of the Conservation Law of the State. Every year fish and game inspectors brought in a sheaf of complaints against fishermen on Long Island for violating the law by taking scallops under one year old. A large number of these cases were scheduled for trial. I went out to Long Island to try them.

There was no question of the guilt of these fishermen. It was easy to establish that they took the young scallops. In each case the fishermen had been caught coming in with their catch, and samples of the scallops had been taken. But in case after case juries disagreed. I just couldn't understand it. Finally, we got to know the jurors pretty well, and after about the fifth or sixth disagreement, I asked some of the jurors about it. They were very frank. "Why, Mr. Attorney General," they said, "there is no question that these men are guilty. We understand the need of conserving fish life and not taking scallops under one year old, but this has been going on for a long time. Now, all of a sudden, the State indicts these small, individual fishermen. Why don't you go after the big oyster companies? We are not going to convict these little fellows. The big companies do the same thing day after day and are never bothered."

On the way home I asked the conservation officials about it. They looked at me and said: "Would you prosecute one of those big companies?" "Of course I would," I said. "It's a violation of the law, isn't it?" "Yes, but—" They sort of hemmed and hawed and said finally that they didn't believe any such action would receive approval "all the way up." They had been in the service many years.

I told them to go out and get the evidence. Within two weeks they had brought in complaints against most of the large oyster companies. They were really large corporations. They owned their own tugs and also owned a large part of the waters from which they took their oysters, clams and scallops. I adjourned all pending cases against the small, private fishermen and went out to try my first big oyster company case.

The company was represented by a prominent lawyer who later became a Supreme Court judge in New York State. He asked for an adjournment, and before I could open my mouth, it was granted. I went out to Riverhead, Long Island, to try this case at least four or five times, and each time adjournment was requested and immediately granted. Finally, after many weeks of these delays, I appeared in court on the date last set for trial, and, much to my surprise, the company was ready for trial.

I had not even adjusted myself at the counsel table, and the first juror had not yet been called, when counsel for the big company addressed the court and requested the court to ask the Attorney General to advise under what section of the law he intended to prosecute. That was easy. The law was not more than one and a half lines long. "No scallops under one year of age shall be taken," was the way it ran. I cited it. Whereupon, the company's counsel, with a happy grin, took a telegram from his pocket and said: "If Your Honor please, that law was changed last night, and I have a telegram from the Governor so informing me. Now, if Your Honor please, inasmuch as this law has been changed, I submit that it would be hardly worth while to continue with this trial. Clearly the legislature has seen the fallacy of such a law."

The judge seemed not a bit surprised. He seemed to know more about it all than I did. "Oh, yes, Counsellor, I quite agree," he said. "Of course, if the Attorney General insists on a trial, I suppose we will have to go through with it, but I quite agree that it will serve no purpose whatsoever." The law had been changed simply by inserting the words "in public waters." The little fisherman caught his fish in public water, while the big companies had leased private waters along the coast!

I did not proceed with the trial, as it would have been useless. But I also did not prosecute any more of the cases against the small fishermen. I learned afterwards that there had been an understanding for many years that the big oyster companies were not to be disturbed. I suppose the same condition exists to this date. Law is all right so long as big interests are not disturbed. It seems it was easier in that case to change the law than to change the Attorney General.

Another time I was given the first case under a new Weights and Measures Law. The law required that the true weight be stated on all food and containers. The first case was against some large packing houses for misstating the weights on hams and bacon. It looked like a very simple case to me. There was no question as to the identity of the hams and bacon. There was no question as to their weight, or that they were underweight. Several ounces underweight made a difference of perhaps five per cent in price.

The State Department of Agriculture was very keen about establishing the efficacy of this new law, for it had taken several years to get it enacted. The violation was a misdemeanor. The case, therefore, was of a criminal nature and was instituted in the Magistrates' Court of the City of New York. When the case was called, my neighbor in Greenwich Village, State Senator James J. Walker, later Mayor, appeared for the defense.

I called my first witness, one of the inspectors of the packers' plants. Whereupon, Senator Walker addressed the court, stating that he was the author of the law, that it was never intended to apply to "wrappers," that the hams and bacon were in wrappers, and not in a container, that the requirement that true weight be shown only applied to containers of glass, wood or tin but did not apply to wrappers. And, of course, he knew, for he had written the bill.

He also knew the judge, who was an affable Tammany judge. He went out of his way to be nice to Jimmy, and my case was dismissed then and there. I started to protest —for all the good it did me! I had known Jimmy for some time, and after the case was dismissed, the judge came out, and Jimmy and the judge invited me to have a drink. I was still protesting at the dismissal of my case. "Jimmy," I said, "how in the world can you possibly appear in a case to defeat your own law?" And Jimmy, in his urbane way, said: "Fiorello, when are you going to get wise? Why do you suppose we introduce bills? We introduce them sometimes just to kill them. Other times we even have to pass a bill. Why are you in the Attorney General's office? You're not going to stay there all your life. You make your connections now, and later on you can pick up a lot of dough defending cases you are now prosecuting." And, of course, the judge acquiesced in all that.

"But," I said, "a lot of little storekeepers have been fined for selling the same kind of hams in wrappers." "Fiorello," said Jimmy, "you stop worrying about those things. What are you in politics for, for love?"

Well, that was the end of the Walker Law so far as the big packers were concerned. When I reported the incident, no one in the department seemed to be shocked. They had run into the same kind of thing in the course of trying to enforce a great many of our laws. Once in a while, a conscientious deputy would proceed with his case, but sooner or later he would find himself blocked, if big interests were involved. Politics, politics, politics! I found very little difference in their philosophy among members of either big party. I was to find the same kind of thing going on after I went to Congress.

But I just could not be a regular. Not to comply and accept the established custom, things as they are, and to raise a howl and kick, brands one as an insurgent. I managed to survive, but many others who bucked the machine during their early careers were through before they could get their start. I enjoyed the work in the Attorney General's office. I left it much wiser and not so innocent as when I entered it.

2

In November 1914, when I ran for Congress the first time and was defeated, there was very little war talk in the United States, though the war in Europe had been going on for four months. War orders were having their stimulating effect on employment, production and business in general, and the country began to pull out of the depression it had been in just before the European nations went to war. While I was serving as Deputy Attorney General in 1915, I became convinced that the situation was serious and decided that I might as well get myself ready for war.

After that fanatical Serbian student had touched off the long-expected European war by hurling a bomb into the carriage of Archduke Franz Ferdinand, the Hapsburg heir to the Austro-Hungarian throne, I could appreciate that this was not just another political assassination. During my consular days I had spent a great deal of time with junior officers of the Austro-Hungarian Army. I knew what had been drilled into them. I also knew the racial and national antagonisms that had caused so much bad feeling for so many years in that part of the world. The officers I had talked with anticipated the day when Europe would be controlled by Teutons. They scoffed at the military weakness of France and Great Britain. The United States, for them, was completely out of the picture.

For most Americans, too, the United States was completely out of the picture. It struck me as strange how casual the interest of the American people was during those hectic days of the summer of 1914, just before hostilities broke out. The newspapers covered the situation quite fully. But our people never seemed to realize that they were going to be affected by what was happening. They lacked knowledge of European political events and economic and political rivalries. Most Americans had a smug self-assurance that they could not possibly become involved and did not realize the magnitude of the conflict. Some of the smarter boys knew that war would provide a market for our goods, food and other material, and some of them realized that war would give us a great advantage over our main competitors for trade, Great Britain and Germany, if it should last long enough to exhaust both of them. As soon as war broke out, I convinced myself that we would become involved, but I could not find any one to agree with me.

After the first shots had been fired, Great Britain wielded great influence on the Italian government to keep it from joining its partners, Germany and Austria, in the Triple Alliance. That was not difficult because of the traditional hatred of the Italian people for Austria, which had seized and was holding what was known as the Italian Unredeemed Provinces, including Trieste. The Italian people were overwhelmingly against participation on the side of Austria and Germany. Italy received definite commitments from Great Britain that if she remained neutral, she would have those Unredeemed Provinces returned to her. When Italy finally entered the war on the side of the Allies in 1915, those commitments were increased.

Not until the Presidential election of 1916 did it dawn on most of the American people that we might get into this war. Our exports had increased enormously. We were selling to both sides at the outset. Germany never succeeded in shutting off our shipments to Great Britain and France and to Mediterranean ports, though the British Navy soon stopped shipments to the Central Powers. Even after Germany stepped up her submarine warfare and declared a blockade of the entire British coast, she was never completely effective in keeping out our supplies. Germany knew our military and naval strength to a man. She had full details of our unpreparedness. The unpleasantness with Mexico in 1916 and our border military activity at that time was not at all impressive in comparison with the might of the armies in European trenches. Germany went as far as she did in submarine warfare because she never could believe that the United States would enter the war. Besides, Germany had many friends in the United States. The German element was rather powerful in American politics, especially in many of the larger cities. Great Britain was not popular in many places in the United States, and Germany did not overlook that situation. We did not know much about propaganda in those days, and we did not realize the extent of German propaganda in the

United States during the first world war. Though we got a liberal education afterwards and are experts at it now, I do not think we were ever as skillful and subtle as the Germans. We ourselves have now reached the point of overdoing our propaganda.

Having convinced myself that we were going to get into the war, I decided that I wanted to go into our Air Corps. I got hold of my friend Giuseppe Bellanca, the brother of my friend August Bellanca, the garment workers' leader. As a boy in Sicily Giuseppe had got interested in aviation, when Santos-Dumont first started to fly there. Bellanca spent hours on the Sicilian beaches scaling flat stones and watching them hop. He carefully watched the birds fly and studied aerodynamics by himself. He managed to get a grounding in higher mathematics. Even as a boy he was always talking about flying.

Giuseppe Bellanca came to this country before the war and started making airplanes by hand. I was the attorney for the company he formed, which consisted of about twenty-five cooks and waiters, each of whom had put in about $100. All of them attended all the meetings of the company, which were quite exciting. I did their legal work free of charge.

Besides building planes, Giuseppe Bellanca ran a small flying school at Mineola, Long Island. It was there that I studied flying. Aviation was young then. Bellanca had two planes. One was used for instruction. It was a light Blériot-type monoplane with a three-cylinder Anzani motor. It was a pretty little toy, but it flew. The motor was supposed to develop about 30 horsepower. If we got fifteen out of it, on actual test, we were doing well.

Quite an assortment of individuals were learning to fly

at this school. We flew irregularly, whenever we had the time, and whenever the wind was right. I taught Bellanca how to run my secondhand Ford, while we were en route to his flying school. Mile-a-Minute Murphy was one of the other pupils. He was a New York City policeman who had made a record a generation before by riding a bicycle at the speed of a mile a minute, paced by a Long Island Railroad train. Bicycles were now too slow for him, so he decided to learn to fly. There was a Chinese, who was always mysterious about himself, and we never did learn where he had turned up from. There was also a Vermont farmer whose aunt was paying his bill and was very eager that he should learn how to do stunt flying. Then there was a young lady who had a perfect wardrobe of flying clothes, but who showed up very seldom for her lessons.

We felt our way and learned to fly like fledgelings. Our first lessons were devoted to what we called grass-cutting. We would sit in the instruction plane for a ground run of about a mile and a half. Then we would get out, turn the plane around and taxi back. It was necessary to control the throttle so that we would not lift off the ground. After we had qualified at doing that and were able to keep the machine straight, the next step was a straightaway hop on the same course. We would lift the machine about 15 to 100 feet in the air and then land. This simple instruction went on for quite a while before we were allowed to circle the field.

The instruction plane had no dual controls. It was a single-seater, and one had to remember what one was told and then trust to luck. After I went through this course, I had got the feel of the air and learned the nomenclature of a plane and the terms used in flying, but I was not much of a flyer. It did help me to get into the Air Corps later, however.

I believed then, as I believe today, that Giuseppe Bellanca is one of the greatest plane designers the world has ever known. He could get more lift out of less horsepower than any plane maker. He always had tough going. He never had enough capital, and many of his associates were always more interested in promotion than in production. Bellanca produced the Columbia plane, built by hand. That type of plane had more crossings of the Atlantic to its credit than any other plane during the early period of trans-Atlantic flying. In fact, the old Columbia is still kicking around somewhere. Bellanca planes of that period won all the efficiency contests at air meets, so much so that the contests were finally eliminated. I actually saw the present multi-motor two-winged monoplane, now of standard type, on Bellanca's drawing-boards back in 1914. During World War II, the Navy took his design, went into production, with not even a word of credit or thanks to Giuseppe Bellanca. Some contractor made a lot of money out of it.

3

I kept pretty busy in 1915 and 1916, what with my work in the Attorney General's office, learning to fly, and building my fences for the 1916 Congressional campaign. I had my heart still set on going to Congress, and my first defeat did not discourage me. Once when I was in Washington, a member of Congress gave me a card to the "family" gallery. I would not go. I did not want to enter the House of Representatives until I could go on the floor as a member. But I read the *Congressional Record* religiously.

That was the easiest part of my preliminary training. The big job was making friends, so that I could win the election.

I knew that I could not depend much on the Republican organization, because of my first experience with it in 1914. It was pretty clear to me that the seat in Congress from my district appeared to belong to the National Liquor Dealers' Association in the name of Michael Farley, the Democratic incumbent, by tacit agreement with the Republicans. But I kept building up my contacts. My law office was a regular Legal Aid Society, and after office hours at the Attorney General's office I made many friends useful to me in politics by going to clambakes, balls, weddings and funerals—functions inseparable from the life of a man in politics. I got to know a great many people in my district.

When the time came for the Congressional nomination in 1916, I was surprised, shocked and hurt to learn that I was not slated for the place on the Republican ticket. I felt I was entitled to it because of the run I had made in the previous election two years before. But that run had attracted a great deal of interest in the nomination. Everybody was nice, giving me good advice about not taking another licking. I was destined, they said, to be a judge or something big like that. "Just be a good boy, go along with the organization, help wherever you can," they told me. That didn't register very well with me.

I got my petitions printed. I was told that was not in the books, that recognition had been given me by my appointment as Deputy Attorney General; I must not hurt my own interest, but just go along and be a good soldier. I insisted that I would contest any nomination made by the party and run in the primaries against another Republican organization choice.

Finally, I made an appointment to see Fred Tanner, who was then Republican State Chairman. He had been leader of my home district. Fred Tanner was a prominent lawyer, scholarly and gentlemanly, who was interested in politics. He had had a meteoric rise in the Republican Party, but he was far too refined and clean to make a success as boss of the New York State Republicans. Naturally, Tanner was greatly occupied, as it was a Presidential year. New York State was going to the Republican convention in Chicago with its Governor, Charles S. Whitman, as its favorite son. I do not believe Fred Tanner was very hot about Whitman.

I had an interesting talk with the State Chairman. He repeated the old gaff about my future in politics, and he tried to convince me that it was to my interest to stay put that year. I was not a bit impressed. He was frank enough to tell me that a young outsider wanted the Congressional nomination badly that year. And this young man's friends had promised to make a substantial contribution to the Republican Party, if he got the nomination. The outsider's name was Hamilton Fish. There is no doubt that he wanted to go to Congress, and he succeeded after World War I. But he was elected to Congress from Dutchess County, a long way from 14th Street in Manhattan.

Fred Tanner made one blunder in his effort to talk me out of running that year. He said that if I had gone to any expense, such as printing my petitions, or anything else, he would see that I was reimbursed. Well, I just hit the ceiling. I don't think Fred meant it the way I took it. But I blew up, and that just about ended our talk.

As I started out of his office, Fred shouted to me, "Fiorello, hold your horses. Damn it, if you want to run, go ahead and do it. Don't blame me if you're licked again."

Harry Andrews was a very useful man around our district. He was young, a good stenographer, did most of the clerical work, and acted as secretary to the district leader. He had a job as a secretary to a judge. In 1914 he was in my corner, and he was very helpful to me in both the primary stage of the 1916 campaign as well as in the election. I got him to study law and had the pleasure of seeing him grow and develop to the point where I appointed him a magistrate when I was Mayor. I learned a great deal about politics from Harry, and he, in turn, I believe, learned some things about government from me.

We got my petitions signed and filed. Though I never got a nod or a word from the Republican Party officials, no opposition developed, much to my surprise, and I entered the primaries unopposed. I did have opposition for the Progressive Party nomination. My friend Ben Marsh, a real liberal and a true progressive, who has been on the right side of many losing causes, was my opponent. I won the Progressive nomination, too, and always had a sort of feeling that Ben voted for me.

The campaign was hot. I got a tremendous start on my opponent, the sitting Congressman. His office-holding had gone to his head, and he was terribly inflated. He seldom showed up at his saloon, and when he did, forgot to treat the boys. He had become a "big shot," and was seldom seen in the district. That would not have been so bad if he had ever done anything in Washington. So I had plenty of material to work on.

This time I did not wait for the party leaders to get me

started. I was 'way ahead of them. The campaign was difficult because my district had such varied interests. The East Side section was interested in economics and the future of Europe; Washington Square, before Greenwich Village had become The Village, was most conservative—for higher tariffs, lower taxes, big business stuff; and the West Side Irish were anti-British and completely Tammanyized.

While I had many friends in the Socialist Party, they waged their fight against me on the East Side. It was their tactics to accept an ultra-conservative rather than a progressive. Tammany was counting on a heavy vote in the West Side section of the district and the solid Little Tim Sullivan Third District on the East Side.

This time my candidacy was not taken by Tammany Hall as the joke it had been to its henchmen two years before. They were in a dilemma. They didn't dare put Mike Farley, their candidate, on the stump. So all sorts of stump speakers were imported into the district. We had a great time with them. I covered every corner in that district, I think. We would start early in the evening, on the West Side, keep going east, and it was not unusual for the last street meeting to end 'way past one o'clock in the morning. Then, to Stuyvesant Hall or some coffee house on the East Side for another hour or two of campaigning.

Tammany was not really worried. They depended on two things: on the Democratic majority usual in that Congressional district, which they considered overwhelming, and on the count. Republican leaders in the West Side districts and in some of the East Side districts were not only weak but untrustworthy and venal. The Republican leader in Little Tim Sullivan's East Side district was an Italian who had made a fortune as a padrone for the Erie

Railroad. He worked very closely with Tammany Hall and would do nothing to incur its displeasure. He always got advice, protection and help from the national Republican administration. He was illiterate, ignorant and arrogant. He didn't even treat his family well. The Tammany leader in the same district was one of the Sullivan clan. Little Tim Sullivan was personally a nice fellow, but as tough a Tammany leader as they came. We prepared for fraud by organizing in this district a corps of volunteer watchers for the count, a precaution I have always taken in my subsequent campaigns.

The fighting Irish were helpful to me in that campaign. I knew more about the history of Ireland than Mike Farley did, and some of the Irish thought Mike Farley had not been anti-English enough. I was greatly aided by a corps of volunteers headed by one who became known as the Irish Joan of Arc. She was a real spellbinder; she was not particularly supporting me; but she was certainly opposing Mike Farley.

In my talks on the East Side I dismembered the Hapsburg Empire and liberated all the subjugated countries under that dynasty almost every night. The funny part of it is that I was not fooling and happened to guess future history correctly.

Charles Evans Hughes was the Republican candidate for President against Woodrow Wilson, running for re-election. Naturally, the interest in the campaign was focussed on the Presidential election, which was a tense and close struggle. In the Republican part of the district, which constituted only a small percentage of the total vote, I had the advantage of the fact that they were all for Hughes and would vote the straight Republican ticket, including me.

Hughes was very popular as a former Governor of New York and a Justice of the United States Supreme Court. We were certain of getting a big vote in that "blue stocking" section of my district, and, in fact, we did very little campaigning there.

We were all pretty tired that last Monday night before election day. We stuck it out at meetings until two o'clock in the morning. We had to get up very early on election day, for we had a job to do. After about three hours' sleep, we covered the two or three lodging houses in the district, flop houses. At five o'clock we visited these, for we knew that Tammany planned to vote the inhabitants in a pack between eight and nine that morning. Our boys were ready with coffee and rolls and doughnuts, so that by the time the Tammany men came around, the flop house inhabitants had already voted. It was the first time in years, some of the old timers remarked, that the guests of these flop houses had voted sober.

We had a little trouble early in the morning when word was spread, allegedly by one of the Republican leaders, "La Guardia hasn't got a chance, so trade votes for Congress for a Republican Assemblyman." We got hold of that leader quickly, took him in the car with us and went from polling place to polling place straightening out that one.

Our real trouble started when the polls closed and the count began. In those days we still had paper ballots. The count was long and tedious. There was ample time and opportunity for marking ballots so that they would be disqualified, for substituting ballots, and every other kind of dirty, dishonest political trick.

I took the toughest district on the waterfront to watch.

This attracted a lot of attention, and finally Charles Culkin, one of the top men in Tammany Hall, who held high office from time to time, and was the Tammany leader of that district, came to the polling place. He gently told me, "Why La Guardia, what are you doing here? You shouldn't be here. Everything is all right." "Everything is not all right," I said, "and what is more, Charlie, you sit here and help me watch this count. There is going to be an honest count, and, if not, someone is going to go to jail, and I mean you, Charlie. You stay here and protect your own district." He did. I took a few precincts even in Charlie Murphy's own home district, although he was then the strong boss of Tammany Hall.

I had all sorts of people watching that district of Charlie Culkin's as well as the other districts. There were school teachers, doctors, business men, longshoremen and some tough guys on our side. In the final count in the district where I was helping to watch, I defeated my Tammany opponent by a very small margin. The Democratic vote in that district was usually five to one against the Republican. Charlie Culkin's jaw dropped. He shook his head and asked me if I was satisfied with the count. "Yes," I said, "as soon as the certificate is signed and turned over to the police." It was.

All through the Democratic districts on the West Side riverfront I was running 'way ahead of the ticket. We knew then that if we could keep up that lead, we would overcome the normal majority for the Democrats. We were going well on the East Side. It, too, was well organized. All of our watchers were instructed to remain on duty until the count was entirely completed, the returns officially signed, and the ballot boxes sealed.

It was about four in the morning before we could get a final count. I had won the election. But it was a good thing we had watched that count carefully, for I won by 357 votes— 7,272 for me, 6,915 for Farley.

I got quite a reception on the East Side. Sam Koenig, who was the Republican county chairman, was genuinely elated at my victory. There is one thing I could always say about Sam Koenig then and during the many years following: if he gave you his word about something, he kept it. I anticipated an enthusiastic reception in other parts of the 14th Congressional District. After all, it was the first time a Republican had been elected to Congress below 14th Street since the foundation of the Republican Party. I particularly thought I would get a riotous reception in my own home district. I never saw such gloom anywhere. The hangers-on at the club hardly nodded to me. Someone was on the telephone in the rear office, assuring the Democratic leader of the district, who was supposed to be his rival, "No, Joe, we didn't double-cross you; we didn't do anything for this fellow. You just can't control him." An apology for my victory is what I heard instead of congratulations! Those are just some of the little things that have made me an incurable insurgent.

I got another lesson in politics from that campaign of 1916. William M. Calder, then a Representative in Congress from a Brooklyn district, was running for United States Senator from New York. There was no sham about Bill Calder. A successful builder and an active member of the House of Representatives for many years, a staunch Republican, most conservative, he made no claims to being a progressive and always remained a real party man. He and I had already become close friends.

Calder was opposed by Robert Bacon, who had been in the State Department for a long time as Assistant Secretary of State. In 1909 he had succeeded Elihu Root as Secretary of State. Mr. Bacon was a partner of J. P. Morgan. There was plenty of money in the primary campaign on the Bacon side. But the boys in our district were for Calder, though the Republican organization seemed to favor Bacon. On primary day the "Bacon boys" went up to party headquarters and came back with plenty of dough. During the early evening hours, Bacon cars came through the district dishing out more money. But the "Bacon boys" were amateurs, and the regular district boys were hard-boiled politicians. They were taking Bacon money, but they were getting Calder votes. Calder carried the district overwhelmingly and won the Republican nomination. I don't know whether the same funny situation went on in other districts, but the final result throughout the State was that Calder was nominated and was elected. That impressed me with the fact which I have insisted on so many times, namely, that money in and of itself just cannot win a campaign. This is not to say that Robert Bacon did not have the qualifications for the high office of United States Senator. In fact, he did. But he just didn't have the political appeal.

It was at this same period that the New York Central and Wall Street were in the habit of dividing the United States Senators from New York between them. At the same time in Pennsylvania, the Pennsylvania Railroad took one Senator and the steel interests the other. But that period was coming to an end in 1916. Later Robert Bacon's son, Robert Bacon, Jr., ran for Congress, after his father's death, from a Long Island district and was elected. He was a gentlemanly, amiable and useful member of the House during the entire time of his service there.

4

Things began to happen fast after the re-election of Woodrow Wilson in 1916 on a "He-kept-us-out-of-war" slogan. Charles E. Hughes had conducted a clean, dignified campaign. That man just could not do anything else, whether as investigator of greedy insurance companies, as a practicing lawyer, governor or judge. A rough-and-tumble campaign against Wilson's "He-kept-us-out-of-war" line might have changed the result. But Hughes would not guarantee that he, too, would keep us out of war. He honestly, frankly and openly stated that only the conditions and events of the future could determine whether we would remain out of war or not. Then, there was the trivial incident whereby, because of bad advice, and a mix-up in his itinerary in California, it was made to appear that his failure to call on Senator Hiram Johnson was an intentional slight. That cost Hughes the small majority in California that was needed to bring Wilson one of the closest victories in American history.

After election day, the pace of events increased rapidly. Again, the Germans misinterpreted the sentiments and character of the American people. The Germans took the result of the election to mean that no matter what they did, this country would not declare war on them. We had many sincere pacifists in the country then. I am not using the word in any derogatory sense. They were men who really believed that the war was no concern of ours, and that it would be of greater value to the world if we re-

mained out of it. No less an official than the Secretary of
State, William Jennings Bryan, felt that way. He resigned
his post after it seemed apparent to him that we were
changing our course and adopting a policy that might lead
to war. In the meantime, British propaganda had not been
idle.

The Germans became bolder. Their blockade of the
British Isles had not been effective. They had to increase
their submarine warfare. Their sinking of the *Lusitania*
in May 1915 with the loss of many prominent people was a
great shock. If we were to retain our self-respect, national
integrity, even sovereignty, it was hard to take that kind of
thing. The Germans were determined to cut off Great
Britain entirely and to curtail our shipments to French
and Mediterranean ports. If they could do those two
things, there seemed no doubt of a German victory. But
this German policy depended for its success on the assumption that the United States would not declare war. President Wilson was determined to see to it that Germany did
not get complete control of the seas.

Her indifference to American rights, her arrogance and
conceit led to Germany's downfall. The German Embassy
in Washington was most active socially, politically and in
sabotage. Von Papen was the brains of the intrigues and
sabotage at the Embassy. He was an educated rascal, un-
scrupulous, ready to stoop to anything to obtain the desired
results. He continued his dirty work, wherever there was
dirty work to be done, until the moment he was sent out
of this country. And he kept up the same kind of thing
during ensuing years, particularly during the Hitler period. How he ever escaped the gallows at the Nuremberg
trials is something that it is most difficult to understand. It

was rumored that great outside influence was brought to bear, not necessarily any improper influence on members of the court. I have heard it stated that it was made clear that Von Papen's conviction would be most distasteful to high ecclesiastical authorities. That man never was any good, and the world would have been better off and hundreds of innocent people would still be alive if he had never existed.

Germany still had many friends in the United States in 1916. Her plans had already gone beyond the defeat of Great Britain and France. She had won considerable prestige in South America. With the defeat of Great Britain, France and Russia, she was sure of control of the Near and Middle East. And with the extension of her influence in South America she would have had the United States at her mercy.

During this period Germany was under these misapprehensions: (1) That the United States would not declare war; (2) that if, by some chance, we should declare war, we could not possibly prepare an army to be of any use in time to keep Britain, France and Russia in the fight; (3) that if we could manage to prepare, we could not transport an army overseas; and (4) that if we did transport our armies, they would not be sufficiently trained and equipped to be of much help. Therefore, Germany became brazen in her attitude, and she started trouble in Mexico, one of her worst errors, so far as arousing the American public against her was concerned.

On January 19, 1917, the German Foreign Minister, Arthur Zimmermann, had written the Minister to Mexico, von Eckhardt, a note transmitted through Count von

Bernstorff, German Ambassador in Washington. The note directed the German Minister to Mexico to propose to the Mexican government an alliance with Germany against the United States, in the event that the United States should enter the war, and informed him that Germany intended to resume submarine warfare. He was authorized to promise the Mexican government financial aid and the restoration to Mexico of Arizona, New Mexico and Texas. Mexico was also to ask Japan to join the new alliance. The Thursday morning newspapers on March 1, 1917, contained an account of this note, which our War Department had intercepted. Its publication caused the greatest sensation throughout the country.

In the meantime, before the Zimmermann note was made public, Count von Bernstorff had been given his passport and was on the way home to Germany. On February 1, 1917, Germany had begun unrestricted submarine warfare after announcing drastic restrictions on American commerce on the seas. On February third, this country had broken off diplomatic relations with Germany and began to arm its merchant ships.

President Wilson called the 65th Congress, to which I had been elected, into extra session, to meet on April second. I was glad to get started. I had had no doubt that I would not have to wait the long thirteen months for a regular session before I went to Congress. I visited Washington often between my election and the meeting of the extra session. Since I was a sort of freak, having been elected on the Republican ticket from such a strong Tammany district, I created some interest, and this gave me the opportunity of meeting the leaders of the House, with whom I afterwards served. I grew very fond of many of them and developed great respect and admiration for them. I entered the House under the rule of courtesy by which members-elect were permitted on the floor. My dream of a lifetime had come true.

CHAPTER VI

Congress in Wartime

1

I LIKED CONGRESS from the very first day. The extra session of the 65th Congress met in accordance with the call of the President on April 2, 1917, at twelve noon. Four hundred and twenty-eight members answered to their names. The House proceeded immediately to its first business, the election of its Speaker.

The tradition of ignoring first termers, known as "freshmen Congressmen," and keeping them silent in their seats was surely broken that year. The control of the House was uncertain. The Republicans and the Democrats had each elected 215 members. There were five independents. Representative Michael F. Conry, a Democrat from New York, had died on March second. The balance of power was very precarious, and so every member's vote became important. The health of every member also was important. The first termers, particularly, received considerable attention, and the political leaders certainly catered to us for our votes in that Speakership contest.

Thomas D. Schall, the blind Representative from Minnesota, a Republican, elected with Farmer-Labor support, made a speech pleading for unity and nominated Champ Clark, of Missouri, the Democratic Party's candidate for Speaker. Champ Clark was as fine a gentleman as ever sat in the House of Representatives. The Republicans named James R. Mann, of Illinois, the greatest parliamentarian of his or any other period. He was every inch a statesman—courageous, able and honest. Mann was pretty hard on young members, had no patience with lazy members. In the preliminary moves the majority shifted from side to side. I voted for James R. Mann. On the final count Champ Clark won with 217 votes against 205 for Mann, two for Frederick H. Gillett and two for Irvine L. Lenroot, with two members merely answering present.

From then on, of course, the Democrats were able to organize the House, elected all the officials, committee chairmen and held the majorities on the committees. Representative Schall was rewarded by assignment to the Committee on Rules. This was exceptional for a first termer, as that was one of the most important committees in the House. There was considerable resentment against him among the Republicans, but he outlived it and was not subjected to the retaliation some of us insurgents suffered later. Mr. Schall went on to the United States Senate on the Republican ticket.

Many of the old timers were still in Congress in 1917, and many men who have become famous since, such as Cordell Hull and Tom Connally, were then members of the House. "Uncle Joe" Cannon was still holding forth and going strong. It was not until after the war that he began to weaken physically. Toward the end his memory was failing, and I heard him make the same speech twice in one day. Naturally, I was strongly prejudiced against "Uncle Joe" Cannon. I had followed the fight on Cannonism with great interest. As Speaker he had ruled the House like a Tsar, and I had great admiration for men like

La Follette, Norris, Murdoch and Beveridge, who had led the fight to oppose Cannon and establish for the first time rules of the House which made it acquire some semblance of a representative body.

I could not help liking "Uncle Joe" personally. He was always cordial to young members, always willing to answer questions, which he did by telling some anecdote. While I was thirty-four years old when I became a member of Congress, I looked younger. Some other members of the House were much younger than I. "Uncle Joe" used to get a great kick out of coming up to me when I happened to be standing in the aisle instead of sitting in my seat and saying, "Boy," and then sending me on some errand. Then he would laugh, appear to be surprised, and say: "Oh, excuse me, I am not in the habit of seeing youngsters here as members." The first time he did it, he asked me to go down to the well and get him a bill. I saw the twinkle in his eye. I fooled him; I went down and got the bill.

From my talks with "Uncle Joe" Cannon I gathered that he was still firmly convinced that the old system of Tsar rule was the best. He couldn't understand why the Speaker shouldn't be the Boss. He predicted that all kinds of dire things would come to pass if the House ruled itself. I could not agree with him. I considered it essential and wholesome for the House to control its own machinery. Under the old system the Speaker had absolute control over every bit of legislation that was passed. A member could not get recognition unless the Speaker wanted to recognize him. That meant that any bill could be kept from consideration if the Speaker did not wish to recognize a member for the purpose of calling up a bill. "For what purpose does the gentleman seek recognition?" the

Speaker would ask. Then if he refused to recognize the member, there was no appeal from his decision. Committees under that system were entirely at the mercy of the Speaker because they just could not get consideration of bills he did not want considered.

The successful fight on Cannonism resulted in new rules for the House. These rules took from the Speaker the power to appoint chairmen of committees and established the seniority system. The new rules provided for a calendar and inaugurated Calendar Wednesdays, when committees took turns and had the right to call up any bill reported. A Committee on Rules was established. It could bring bills to the consideration of the House out of their regular order. Priority and precedence for appropriation bills and bills from the Ways and Means Committee were established. The Unanimous Consent Calendar was provided for, a system by which non-controversial bills could be expeditiously passed by unanimous consent. In short, the House of Representatives became potentially what it should be, a body of representatives of the American people, with a voice in the enactment of legislation, possessing reasonable assurance that their legislation could be properly considered. This was quite an improvement and was successful for some years. But, then, even these modernizations became archaic. It fell to my lot in 1924 to lead a new movement for further liberalization of the House rules.

2

The one thought in Congress in April 1917 was war. We had finished organizing ourselves in the House at 7:47 of the evening of April second. Then the Senate and the

House met again at 8:30 in the House chamber to hear President Wilson deliver his message. Though we had already broken off diplomatic relations with Germany, there were still some members of Congress who thought that President Wilson would not ask for a declaration of war. Had a vote been taken before Wilson's forceful and persuasive message, I am not sure that a majority could have been obtained for that declaration. The propaganda was something terrific. Groups of every kind were pouring into Washington. The corridors of the House Office Building and of the Capitol were jammed. Telegrams and mail poured in so heavily that it was impossible to open or read all the messages. Everyone that any member ever knew seemed to have been approached by someone and wrote in, either for a declaration of war or against it.

The House was very restive. The situation was tense. President Wilson looked serious and determined. He read his message beautifully, pausing after he made a point, emphasizing clearly what he wanted to get across. It was a magnificent presentation.

The President pointed out that, as he had informed the Congress on February third, the Imperial German government had announced its intention on and after the first of February to use its submarines to sink on sight every vessel approaching Great Britain or the ports controlled by Germany's enemies. Wilson called this "a warfare against mankind." He had in his message to Congress of February twenty-sixth advocated a policy of "armed neutrality." But, he said, that policy was now impracticable, because the German government intended to regard our armed guards on our merchant ships as pirates. He asked that the Congress accept a state of war against Germany, and that it take immediate steps to put the country in a state to prosecute that war effectively. He told the Congress that we had no quarrel with the Germans, but only with their aggressive rulers. He welcomed the Russian people into a "league of honor" of free peoples and praised them for throwing off, a few weeks before, the shackles of autocracy by revolution. He recalled the fact that the Prussian autocracy had filled our country with its spies and had tried to arouse our neighbor, Mexico, against us. We were fighting, he said, for the liberation of peoples, including the German peoples, for the rights of nations great and small. "The world must be made safe for democracy," he added.

In his Inaugural Address about a month before, President Wilson had said: "We are provincials no longer. The tragical events of the thirty months of vital turmoil through which we have just passed have made us citizens of the world. There can be no turning back. Our own fortunes as a nation are involved, whether we would have it so or not."

The House adjourned after we heard the President's message. Next day, the Committee on Foreign Affairs reported a resolution declaring war on Germany. The debate started. It was heated, at times bitter. The Chicago and Wisconsin delegations in the House were strongly opposed to the declaration of war. The debate continued for several days. Sessions were long, and a number of night sessions were held. The galleries were packed all the time.

Our debate ran on into Thursday, April fifth, and after a short recess we resumed in night session. Every member who wanted to talk had the opportunity to take the floor. Debate was absolutely unlimited and no member was gagged. It was past midnight, and now Good Friday, 1917. Before the previous question was called, which would close the debate and start the vote, Representative Murray Hulbert, of New York City, a devout Catholic, made a plea for the House to adjourn until Monday, or at least Saturday, so that war would not be declared on Good Friday. He was earnest and quite emotional. Tears rolled down his cheeks. The gentleman's motion to adjourn was voted down.

Then Representative Fred A. Britten, of Illinois, offered a motion to recommit the declaration of war to the Committee on Foreign Affairs for amendment to provide that no forces of the United States be sent to Europe, Asia or Africa until Congress specifically directed that they be sent there, unless they were volunteers. Mr. Britten's motion was voted down by a voice vote. It was my belief at the time, and I have talked it over with a great many of my colleagues since, that at least sixty to sixty-five per cent of the members who voted for war did so in the belief and firm conviction that we would never have to send a single soldier to Europe. It was believed generally in the country at the time that all we would be called upon to do and all that would be needed was to provide our Allies with funds, ammunition and other supplies, stop all shipments to Germany or to countries friendly with Germany, and the mighty military force of Imperial Germany would collapse. Many members of the House were certainly of that opinion.

Finally, around three o'clock in the morning, the vote was put to the House. The roll call began. The clerk read the names slowly. Every member was in his seat. "Yes," "Aye," and an occasional "No" resounded solemnly in the tense chamber. The clerk reached the R's, and Jeannette

Rankin's name was called. It was a firm and unbroken rule of the House that no comment or explanation could be made during a roll call. It was either "Yes" or "No." Then Jeannette Rankin broke a precedent of 140 years and said, "I want to stand by my country, but I cannot vote for war." There was a hush. The reading clerk turned to the Speaker. Tally clerks awaited instructions. "Continue the call," said Champ Clark, and Miss Rankin was recorded in the negative. It was stated at the time that Miss Rankin was crying. I have been asked the question so many times. I do not know, for I could not see because of the tears in my own eyes.

That House appreciated the enormity of the action we were taking. The final vote was 373 for war, 50 against, 9 not voting. At 3:14 A.M. on Good Friday the House adjourned, and the United States had officially entered World War I.

3

There was not much for us to do when the House reconvened Monday, April ninth. For several days there was a complete let-down after the tenseness and excitement of the declaration of war. None of us new members of Congress was appointed to any of the important committees, so we had plenty of time on our hands at a time when we wanted to be up and doing. The Ways and Means Committee was considering the foreign loan bill. The Military Affairs Committee had several important bills before it, including the aviation bill.

We had no air service at that time. Though the European war had been going on for nearly three years, and aviation had developed from an incidental agent of observation to an indispensable means of observation as well as a force for bombing and "strafing," the United States did not have a single, solitary modern fighting plane or anything that could then be sent into action. Our aviation was still part of the Army's Signal Corps, and the Air Service did not come into existence until many months later. Our first aviation bill authorized the expenditure of $640,000,000 for equipment.

The country responded quickly and enthusiastically to the call for war. But there was as yet very little talk of an expeditionary force. Germany was stunned. Great Britain, France, Italy and Russia took on new hope, even though they were in a bad fix. The foreign missions, headed by Joffre and Balfour arrived in Washington. General Joffre pleaded with President Wilson for troops, troops and more troops, and we began suddenly to realize that we were in a war in which we would carry grave duties and responsibilities. Joffre made it clear that the Germans could not be beaten except by a great superiority of armed forces. France was rapidly becoming exhausted; Great Britain had reached almost the limit of replacements; Italy had all she could do to hold her line; Russia was disrupted by defeat and internal disorder.

President Wilson was convinced of the great need for an American expeditionary force. So was the War Department. The President called a conference of the chairmen and ranking members of the Senate and House Military Affairs Committees at the White House. I learned that it was a stormy meeting. President Wilson presented the case for an expeditionary force to go to France as soon as possible. He asked for a draft law calling upon all young Americans to share in the responsibility. And he met opposition. He was firm. He had given the matter much thought, and he knew very well that a draft was necessary sooner or later, that if it came later, the flower of American manpower would already have responded and might well have been wiped out, as had happened in Great Britain. In order to obtain the necessary number of men as soon as they were needed, to provide proper large scale training, there was only one way, and that was to commence drafting men at once.

The War Department worked frantically on a draft bill. Then it was sent to the House Military Affairs Committee, which was under the control of the Democrats. Chairman Dent, head of that committee, was opposed to the draft, and so was the second-ranking member of that committee. It fell to Representative Julius Kahn, of California, the ranking minority member, to sponsor the draft bill on the floor of the House and to fight it through to success. He assumed that great responsibility and performed it beautifully. It was one of the hardest fights anyone sponsoring a bill had ever had to wage in the history of the House. The Speaker, the majority leader, the chairman of the Military Affairs Committee all were against the draft bill. They fought it openly and vigorously. It was during that debate that Speaker Champ Clark referred to "conscript or convict" in his famous speech on the subject. While the debate was going on, the Army pulled one of its boners by advertising for recruits, using sensational posters with the legend, "Don't be a Sent, be a Went." That certainly didn't help matters any. Those of us in the House who were fighting for the bill compelled the War Department to withdraw those posters quickly.

Fred Britten, of Illinois, who when he became chairman

of the Naval Affairs Committee after the war, was one of the greatest fire-eating militarists in the House, fought the draft bill to the very end. He had also voted against the declaration of war. Freddie had a German constituency.

During the debate, some member who had the floor, talking in opposition to the draft, asked how many members of the House who were going to vote to send boys to war would go themselves. Five of us stood up: Gardner, who went early and died after a few months; Haskell, who reported for active service with his National Guard regiment but could not stand the physical strain and returned to the House; Heintz; Johnson, of South Dakota, and myself. Three of us got into active combat service. Royal Johnson was badly wounded toward the end of the war.

Finally, on April twenty-eighth, the draft bill passed the House by a vote of 397 to 24. It had tough sledding in the Senate but was finally passed there too. During the weeks of debate before a draft bill succeeded, the War Department did an excellent job of making all necessary preparatory plans for conscription. It was able to snap into action a few days after the bill became a law. Hugh Johnson, later famous as "Iron Pants," was one of the chief organizers of the draft under our great Secretary of War, Newton D. Baker, and the Chief of Staff, Peyton C. Marsh, who was a great organizer. It was my impression that the administration of the draft law in the first world war was smoother and better than in World War II. But, of course, the number of men called was not nearly so great then, and there was not the same degree of necessary dislocation as was caused by Selective Service during World War II.

I did not believe that anyone should be exempted from the draft even for conscientious or religious objections to war. I offered an amendment to the draft bill providing for no exemptions but permitting those with honest, conscientious objections or religious convictions to be excused only from combat service. I wanted them to be assigned to clerical, hospital, agricultural or manual work of a noncombatant nature. My amendment was defeated. I was even against exemptions for physical deficiencies if those people could perform clerical or other less strenuous work than field or combat service. I was also opposed to any young man holding officer's rank during the first six months of his service, so that all would be trained on a basis of absolute equality, and we would have a really democratic army.

During the early days of my service in the House, I sent post cards to my constituents in the 14th Congressional District asking for their opinions on conscription and explaining that it treated everyone alike, subject only to age and physical qualifications. I wrote my constituents:

"I think conscription is needed, and I am trying to educate the people up to it. There have been attempts to introduce bills into Congress which would exempt the farmer from service, or the cotton grower, or the tobacco grower. If New York does not watch out she will be having to supply as large a proportion of the Army as she now does of the taxes, which is one-third. The only way to avoid this is to institute compulsory service. It is up to you to respond; don't blame me if you don't like the way I vote."

Quite a few of my constituents did not like my vote in favor of the draft bill. There were Socialists and others in my district opposing the war. But I started then the policy I used ever afterwards of voting as I thought right, explaining my views frankly to my constituents, and taking the consequences.

Even before the declaration of war on April sixteenth, I had introduced my first bill in Congress. On April third, the day after the House convened in the 65th Congress, I offered H.R. 345. It made the fraudulent sale of war materials a felony punishable by imprisonment in time of peace and by death in time of war. It was referred to the Committee on the Judiciary, where it reposed. I was thinking of my father's experience during the Spanish-American War, when the condemned beef he had eaten because of the negligence and irresponsibility of corrupt Army contractors, had caused his disability and finally his death. I wanted to protect the boys who were being conscripted from the dangers of corrupt practices at home while they were fighting abroad.

4

Next to the conscription bill the measure of greatest importance before the House was the foreign loan bill. It was the first time in the history of the United States that the House of Representatives had juggled billions. The bill was presented as a pure, unadulterated loan and called for $3,000,000,000. Our Allies were in need of the money. It was our duty to lend it. We were assured that it would cost the United States nothing, inasmuch as the money would be returned with interest in full, so that the bonds would never be a burden to the American taxpayer. And we were told that it would save thousands and thousands of American boys' lives. These assurances and promises were received from the President, the Secretary of the Treasury, the chairman of the House Ways and Means Committee,

and member after member who got up on the floor to
argue for the foreign loan bill.

On April fourteenth I told the House:

"I do not share the belief of some of my colleagues who
have expressed firm confidence and figure on the complete
restitution of the $3,000,000,000 loan to be made to for-
eign governments. Yes; I believe that a good portion will
be in due time returned, but I am certain that some of it
will have to be placed on the profit and loss column of
Uncle Sam's books. Let us understand that clearly now
and not be deceived later. Even so, if this brings about a
speedy termination of the European war and permanent
peace to our own country it is a good investment at that."

I wanted to vote for foreign loans, but I did not want
Congress and the country to kid themselves about getting
the money back with interest in full and then being disappointed and bitter about it. At the time, my speech was
regarded as just another crack from a rookie member.
But it has been quoted often since, during the refunding
negotiations in later years and after defaults and subsequent loan transactions with our Allies.

When these refunding negotiations were on, I took part
in the debate. There was opposition to refunding on any
basis but the full principal and interest. I told the House:
"Take it. Be lucky if you get it at all. I doubt that you
will get even this much." Next to Finland, Great Britain
had the best record so far as our World War I debt was
concerned. The loans of World War I had to be greatly
reduced and are not paid in full today. Lend lease was
quite properly marked off to the greatest extent. Had it
not been for Great Britain holding the line, we would
have been paying big indemnities to the Nazis at this very

moment, and I would never have been writing these memoirs.

As to the loan of $3,750,000,000 in 1946 to Great Britain, we might as well know now, as we should have known in 1917 about our war loans, that it cannot be paid back in the time set and according to the terms of the agreement. There is no use predicting when or how much will be paid. None of us alive today will live to see that loan paid in full.

War measure after war measure began to come before the House for consideration. Congress got more eager, and even bloodthirsty. Members who had been timid during the opening days of the session were now shouting the loudest and demanding more and more drastic measures. The rights of individuals who could be falsely accused of impeding the war effort by over-eager legislative warriors had to be protected. At least, someone had to make an attempt to curb hysteria so that we did not destroy, in the war we were engaged in, the rights we were anxious to preserve.

The feeling against our entering the war had acquired considerable momentum and could not be stopped immediately after the declaration of war. There were sincere and honest men who were pacifists. By no means all of our pacifists were pro-Germans. There was some anti-British feeling in New England. The Germans took full advantage of conflicts in sentiment and organized all sorts of anti-war activities and sabotage plots. There was obvious need for security measures.

I felt at the time that the espionage bill as originally introduced into Congress was too severe. It could be used to cause abuses of individual liberty and contained possibilities of persecution and miscarriages of justice. I sought to put some sense into the measure. While some changes were made in the original measure, the bill as finally passed contained many of the evil provisions, and many of the injustices I had feared actually occurred.

Some provisions of the espionage bill, I felt, would prevent legitimate criticism of maladministration in the military establishment and the government in general. Such criticism was not necessarily of advantage to the enemy and lack of it could be of great disadvantage to our own efficiency. The ban on the right to indulge in it would deprive American citizens of their traditional privilege to criticize their government even in military affairs. I was also worried that some provisions of the espionage bill might prevent legitimate aid being given to republican movements in European countries by citizens of the United States.

I received time to talk on the espionage bill on May 2, 1917. I objected to the fact that while time had been unlimited for debate on the resolution declaring war and on the conscription bill, an attempt was being made by the sponsor of the espionage bill, Mr. Webb, of North Carolina, a member of the House Judiciary Committee, to limit debate to five minutes for any member. "No member of this House," I said, "should be limited in his opposition to this un-American and vicious legislation."

"This bill," I told the House, "is the most important measure that has come before the House during this and many previous sessions. It is a revolutionary measure. It shocks me as much as if a bill were proposed to change the color and formation of that flag we so dearly love. Gentlemen, if you pass this bill and if it is enacted into law you change all that our flag ever stood and stands for, even though we do not change her colors. . . . This country will continue to exist after this war, and I want to do my part that it may exist a free and independent nation, a Republic of republics, a model and inspiration to the oppressed people of the world.

"We all have our heart and soul in this war, but because we have our heart in it is no reason why we should lose our head. . . . We have the responsibility of carrying this country through this war without impairing or limiting any of her institutions of true liberty or losing her entity as an ideal Republic."

Of course, I did not object to any provisions of the espionage bill that guarded against the activities of spies. But I objected most to Section 4, which deprived our own citizens of their liberties. Under that section the President was permitted to prohibit publication or communication of *any* information relating to the "national defense." That term "national defense" embraced reference to "any person, place, or thing in any wise having to do with the preparation for or the consideration or execution of any military or naval plans, expeditions, orders, supplies, or warfare for the advantage, defense or security of the United States of America." Discussion of any such matters could subject a citizen to imprisonment for ten years. I maintained that this section violated Article 1 of the First Amendment to the Constitution, part of our invaluable Bill of Rights. Under that Section 4, any critic of inadequacy of food, contract frauds, of inefficiencies in the War Department, could be put in jail, and I offered to draw an indictment to prove it.

"The people of this country are united in their demand

that the scandals, abuses, graft and incompetency of 1898 are not to be repeated," I told the House, "and the press is their medium of detecting and exposing these abuses and crimes. It is our duty as their representatives to do nothing which will impair, restrict, or limit the press in the fulfillment of that duty. This alone, without considering the destruction of one of our basic fundamental principles of liberty, is sufficient justification to arouse the indignation of this House and send this bill back to the committee, where it should die in shame and neglect."

I recalled that the infamous Sedition Act of 1798 was the last previous attempt to shackle the minds of the American people in the way we were trying to do it in 1917. I also pointed out that under the provisions of this espionage bill assistance to oppressed peoples in other parts of the world would be prevented, and if such an act had been on our statute books at the time, the Republic of Portugal would not have seen the light and the hopes of the Russian people would not have been realized.

On May fourth the House voted to strike out the whole of the dangerous Section 4 by a vote of 221 to 167. I voted against the espionage bill as a whole even with the offensive Section 4 removed because I thought it still contained too many dangerous provisions. The act was passed and remained on our statute books, a potential danger to our liberties thereafter. On February 9, 1931, I wrote to Norman Thomas in answer to a letter from him asking me to vote for repeal of the Espionage Act, which the Senate had voted unanimously to repeal:

"Please do not talk repeal of the Espionage Act to me. I introduced a bill for its repeal in 1919 and every Congress thereafter. We just cannot get anywhere with it. It is most discouraging. The old argument that it is effective only in event of an emergency and, therefore, not hurting any one now will be renewed with added emphasis at this time. . . . Frankly, I do not believe we can get any action on the repeal at this session of Congress." *

People convicted under the Espionage Act during the war were deprived of their rights as citizens because of their utterance of criticism. I worked with the American Civil Liberties Union to have those rights of citizenship restored to them, but the Hoover administration opposed any such move. More than ten years after the war had ended, 1,500 men and women, convicted under the Espionage Act, for their utterances, were still deprived of the right to vote, serve on juries or hold public office. In some States they could not obtain licenses to practice professions or engage in some trades, or even get licenses to run automobiles or go hunting and fishing. Many of the culprits had merely made remarks opposing the war in private conversations. None of these cases involved acts of violence against the government during its war effort. Spies were convicted under other laws. Aliens who were convicted under this Espionage Act were deported after release from prison, and some of them were offered the bargain of short prison sentences if they would accept deportation after serving those sentences. The aliens who chose to take the long sentences instead were later pardoned and permitted to remain in the country. Pacifists, Socialists and I.W.W. migratory workers constituted the majority of those con-

* The Espionage Act never has been repealed but is in effect whenever the United States is actually engaged in war.

victed under the Espionage Act, and among those convicted were Eugene V. Debs and "Big Bill" Haywood.*

Other measures considered by the House during those first months of war contained provisions I considered dangerous to our civil liberties. One provision of the Trading with the Enemy Act permitted the President by proclamation to include in the term "enemy" almost anyone he saw fit. I spoke against that provision, maintaining that it was unnecessary to give the President such powers and pernicious to do so. Our penal laws covered such acts as might be committed by individuals. I pointed out that under this provision a whole class of individuals could be denominated "enemy" and "alien" when there was no evidence sufficient to warrant indictments against them but merely suspicions concerning them. They could be deprived of their right of habeas corpus and their other sacred rights under the law on the say-so of the President or any other officer of the government, to whom he might delegate his broad authority.

We had already passed plenty of acts providing ample protection for the government from enemy aliens or other enemies. Conspiring against the draft was punishable and so was imparting information to the enemy. "This is the first time in the history of this country," I pointed out to the House, "that we have included 'classes' in a bill. We are giving power to take people by class and groups, without trial, without jurisdiction, without showing cause, without proper cause, and hold them until the termination of the war." These broad powers permitted irresponsible

* Amnesty was finally granted these men and women convicted under the Espionage Act and their civil rights restored only after President Franklin D. Roosevelt granted it on Christmas Day, 1933, his first Christmas Day in office.

officials to indict innocent people in time of labor strife or other difficulties just because they may have mailed letters to relatives abroad of enemy nationality. Under this act, enemy aliens might even have been deprived of buying food or using a street car if some official wanted to interpret the law that way. My amendments altering these broad powers of the Trading with the Enemy Act were rejected during this period when zeal and fervor were not always properly channelled.

I also objected without success to a provision in the act giving the federal government large powers over the railroads during the war. That provision gave the President authority to order the armed forces into any locality without first consulting the local authorities under any circumstances the President thought fit. There was absolutely no necessity for this provision. Under it an inexperienced, excitable or ignorant United States marshal could ask the President for use of the armed forces and get it. It was a vicious precedent to establish, and it was part of what I called the "goulash legislation" we were passing in that first wartime session of Congress. Almost every war measure carried in it pet fads and hobbies of some members of Congress.

The number of civilian jobs we were creating by our acts of Congress was enormous. I made every effort I could to have as many of these jobs as possible subject to our Civil Service regulations, whenever that could be done without any hindrance to the war effort. There was great danger that our whole system of appointment by Civil Service examination and under Civil Service regulation would be broken down if we allowed the excuse of war emergency to be used for that purpose by greedy politicians. There were plenty of cases where the excuse that we could not wait for such a thing as a Civil Service examination was being used to get political henchmen jobs whether or not they were qualified for the work. A big food survey was ordered by act of Congress. I succeeded in getting an amendment passed providing that the jobs created under that survey should come under Civil Service, after I had read a letter from J. A. McIlhenny, President of the Civil Service Commission, assuring us that his organization could handle the job without any delay. But I failed in a similar effort to prevent exemption from Civil Service regulations for the large increase in the personnel of the Bureau of Mines to handle our greatly expanded explosives production. Democratic Congressmen then in the majority wanted as many "deserving Democrats" as possible to get those jobs, no matter what their abilities or qualifications.

The food situation was not handled as well during World War I as during World War II. Prices soared beyond the pocketbooks of many families. Many people were not getting enough to eat, though everyone knew that there was plenty of food available, that warehouses and cold storage plants were bulging with it. I pointed out to the House that in a land able to appropriate billions of dollars, with full employment throughout the country, we were witnessing the spectacle of food riots in New York City because women were desperate at their inability to provide their families with adequate nourishment, even though some of them as well as their husbands were wage-earners. Profiteers were amassing great fortunes at the expense of the health and happiness of the American people.

Some doubts were expressed on the floor of the House

about the constitutionality of a national food control bill. It was my view that the far-sighted, liberty-loving men who worked on the Constitution and the Bill of Rights just couldn't imagine that the day would ever come in this country when food would be cornered, or else they would have made provision to assure to every American willing to work the right to food and shelter and clothing among his inalienable rights.

I introduced a Constitutional amendment giving the federal government power at all times to regulate and control the production, conservation and distribution of food supplies. But it got no farther than my bill providing the death penalty in time of war for corrupt contractors. Some day we will come to realize that the right to food, shelter and clothing at reasonable prices is as much an inalienable right as the right to life, liberty and the pursuit of happiness.

The war revenue bill, the largest tax bill in our history up to that time, contained inequities. I tried to get income tax exemptions raised from $1,000 to $1,500 for a single man and from $2,000 to $2,500 for a married man, but I failed. There were taxes on coffee and tea but none on substitutes for them, some of which, I claimed, were spurious, and even injurious to our health. Their freedom from taxes was bound to increase their use, but the House rejected my amendment subjecting them to equal taxes with coffee and tea. I did manage to get an amendment passed bringing under the ten per cent admission tax boxes at opera houses and other places of amusement, also subscription and season tickets. Otherwise, only people in the orchestra, gallery and cheaper seats would have paid taxes. I also tried to have candy selling for thirty cents or less a package, bought by children of poorer families, exempted from taxes, but I failed that time.

When the aviation bill came before the House, there was no opposition to it though it called for the largest amount, $640,000,000, ever appropriated up to that time for any one branch of the Army. It also gave wide, blanket, unprecedented authority for the expenditure of that large sum.

The entire job of designing, producing and delivering planes for war purposes during World War I was a miserable failure and cannot be compared with the magnificent job done during World War II. Considerable study was made by ostensibly qualified technicians. Then the whole aviation program was centered around the Liberty motor. But by the time these studies had been completed and the report based on them accepted, the Liberty motor was obsolete and antiquated. Yet we went right on into manufacture of these Liberties on a big scale. Our decision to build our planes around the Liberty motor was a great disappointment to our Allies, Great Britain, France and Italy. They knew, even in those days, the huge productive capacity of our country. They realized that if it was properly applied, we could surpass the combined efforts of all the Allied countries. It was their hope that we could get into airplane motor production here, where we had so much raw material and manufacturing skill, to such an extent that we could relieve European centers of any further plane production. But the Liberty motor was not only a sad disappointment, but a definite discouragement. Italy had to continue building Fiat and Isotta-Fraschini motors, and France and Great Britain had to go on making their own types. We were responsible for the necessity to use a large part of very scarce shipping tonnage to carry raw materials to them for these airplane motors.

An infinitesimal percentage of Liberty motors got into real action. None that I know of was used by our Allies. Yet we continued to produce them in large numbers. A few American DH-4's did get across. Some were used for observation, some for light bombing. The boys did not like them. They soon got the name "Flying Coffin," and the Liberty motor was considered a jinx. I fully expected a scandal to break over this Liberty motor equal to the scandal over rotten beef during the Spanish-American war. It didn't. A lot of people were lucky. Even after the war, with every single flyer in the Air Service from General Billy Mitchell down knowing the Liberty's faults, the greed went right on. Some powerful interests were involved.

After I had returned to the House from my war service, I found a plan—strangely enough coming from the War Department—to appropriate for the purchase of another 10,000 Liberty motors. The boys in the Air Service were hot under the collar. They kept me well informed. They knew that some influence was working somewhere to put over those additional Liberties. The idea had not come from the Air Service. They already had thousands of these motors lying around the country.

I started to kick up a row. It was said that these Liberties would be useful in the event of another war. We were told that we would never be caught again with an airplane shortage if we had those 10,000 additional Liberties, packed in oil and held in reserve. It sounded good. So sure were General Motors and other companies who had contracts to make Liberties that they were going to get new contracts, that they went right on turning out these motors. I introduced a resolution of inquiry—a tremendously useful legislative weapon, very seldom used. The resolution is highly technical and unless properly drawn can be thrown out on a point of order. If, however, it does survive, it is privileged after eight days, and the House is compelled to vote on it.

My resolution asked that the War Department inform the House of the number of Liberty motors on hand, on order, belonging to the War Department, with the number of each motor. I had a tough time, but I finally got the resolution through. The demand for the 10,000 new Liberty motors seemed suddenly to die. Finally, the report came in, the answer to my inquiry. It was one thick volume with just columns and columns of numbers of Liberty motors. That was the end of the 10,000 new Liberty motors deal, and it saved the country several millions of dollars. The Liberty motor gang were something more than sore. Later on, there were some investigations of their activities, but nothing ever came of them, for there were just too many people with good connections involved in Liberty motor production.

There was a tendency in 1917 on the part of some members of the House to pooh-pooh the airplane and regard it as a mere experiment or a toy. There was also a tendency on the part of others to regard it as a miracle weapon that would win the war. I argued against both attitudes. I told the House that I considered the airplane's usefulness in war was clearly established, and that aviation was, in fact, the most useful branch of the Army. But I had no illusions that aviation would win the war. There was a lot of tough ground fighting and artillery bombardment necessary as well.

The draft act, the foreign loan and trading with the enemy acts, the espionage laws, the food and aviation bills were out of the way by the beginning of July. I became very restive. I had told the young men in my district that if I should vote for putting them into the Army, I would go myself, and personally I was eager to get into action. I was thirty-four years old, physically fit but too short to become a foot soldier. Whatever further war measures might be needed could easily pass the House without my vote. So I was ready to go to the front and determined to do so.

CHAPTER VII

On Active Service

1

ONE AFTERNOON about the middle of July 1917 I went down to the Southern Railway Building in Washington, where the Aviation Section of the Signal Corps was recruiting. I never saw such a collection of applicants: young, cleancut college boys who had heard about flying but knew nothing about it; acrobats and tumblers who thought that because they were good on the tightrope and trapeze, they would be able to fly; and a large miscellaneous group of boys without the necessary educational background who were eager to get into the war, and the quicker the better.

I made out an application blank along with the rest. These blanks were given a quick scanning, and if the applicant seemed to have some qualifications, he was given a medical examination. I passed those two hurdles all right. Then came a test before one of the higher officers. I was turned over to Major W. A. Larned, the tennis champion, a fine, cordial gentleman who later ended his life tragically by suicide.

I had put nothing on my application blank to indicate that I was a member of Congress. Major Larned was impressed by the fact that I had had some little flying training in 1915, but he didn't think much of lawyers as material for the Air Service. He asked me if I would accept a lieutenant's commission, and I told him that I would accept any commission so long as I could fly. After he had approved my application and while I was about to leave, he suddenly called me back to ask me the extent of my knowledge of foreign languages. He had a special form on which he recorded those facts. Then he asked me if I could be ready for active service within a few days. I told him I would be ready at any time. I was hopeful that I would be accepted, and left the old building feeling very happy.

I did not tell anybody about my application except Representative Julius Kahn, member of the House from California, for whom I had great respect and admiration. He agreed with me that nothing should be said about it until I actually received my commission.

Within a very few days, I received a letter asking me to report for active duty within a week, if I could do so, and to report at the Aviation Section in Washington at the earliest possible time. I called that afternoon. I was asked about my knowledge of Italian. Plans were under way for sending aviation cadets to Italy for training, and my knowledge of Italian would be helpful to that enterprise. I seemed to qualify for this special requirement, and I was taken to see Major Benjamin Foulois, Chief of the Air Service. He gave me more particulars about the training program in Italy and told me that we would receive our preliminary training there with some advanced training in bombing for some of the men. The picked contingent of 150 men would be the first to be sent to Italy and was scheduled to leave within about two weeks.

Major Foulois had had considerable contact with Congress when he was helping to get the aviation bill passed and was familiar with the names of members, particularly those who had taken an active interest in supporting the bill. He asked me if I was related to Congressman La Guardia. I asked him if that would make any difference one way or the other. "No, not at all," he said. I asked him if there would be any prejudice against a member of Congress or a member of a Congressman's family being commissioned, or if such action would require special approval from higher up. He said that their need was very urgent, and such approval would not be necessary, that the Air Service would be only too happy to get the right man for the right place. I then told him that I was the Congressman, but that I did not want anything said about it until I got overseas. He said he would forget it.

I was certain in my own mind that precedents were ample against a man holding a seat in Congress and a commission in the Army at the same time. But I felt that it would be good for Congress and good for the Army to have some of us serving abroad, for it would provide a wholesome liaison and do away with a great deal of grousing about Congressmen sending others to war but not going themselves. Congress was bound to be better informed about the war if some of its members served. Members of the British Parliament were serving with the armed forces and retaining their seats.

Representative John Q. Tilson, member of Congress from New Haven, Connecticut, had gone to the Mexican border in 1916 with the National Guard and retained his seat in Congress. I talked the matter over with Colonel Tilson when I was getting ready to join up. He advised me that if I felt I should go into the Army, I should simply do so, and that if both sides of the House agreed with me,

the issue would never be raised. Representative Augustus
P. Gardner, of Massachusetts, son-in-law of Senator Henry
Cabot Lodge, had resigned his seat in Congress in 1917 to
become a major in the Quartermaster Corps. Representative Victor Heintz, of Ohio, went into a Cincinnati regiment and retained his seat, as did Representative Royal C.
Johnson when he enlisted and went to an officers' training
camp. Finally, Representative McLemore, of Texas, introduced a bill in the House granting me a leave of absence
while I was in the Army, so that I would not have to re-
sign my seat. His resolution was referred to the Committee on Elections, but no definite ruling was ever obtained
on the basic problem involved.

Incidentally, during the time when I was Director of
Civilian Defense in World War II and sat in President
Roosevelt's Cabinet, the matter of Congressmen going into
the armed services and retaining their seats came up for
discussion. President Roosevelt asked Attorney General
Biddle to look into the matter. I told him the precedents
following the Civil War, which I had looked up and which
seemed to be against the practice, and of my own experience in World War I. I pointed out that it seemed to depend on what he would like to have for the answer. The
President was amused and, turning to Mr. Biddle, said: "I
guess we will let it go for the present, Francis."

The sergeant-at-arms of the House, on the advice of attorneys, decided that I was not entitled to draw pay as a
Congressman while in the Army. My pay as a Congressman was $7,500 a year, and as a first lieutenant $2,000.
Under this ruling I could not draw pay for my Congressional attachés or for myself. I arranged with the Riggs National Bank in Washington to give me a drawing account,

not to exceed my military pay, with my rights to both Congressional insurance and military risk insurance assigned to the bank. That was the way I financed myself. During the closing days of the special session of the 66th Congress, we Congressmen who had gone to war were voted our pay, so it turned out all right in the end.

I received my commission as a first lieutenant in the Aviation Section of the Signal Corps on August 16, 1917, and was ordered to Mineola, Long Island, a point of embarkation for the Air Service. There I met Major Leslie McDill, commanding officer of our contingent, an alert, intelligent, handsome young officer.

Our first problem was to assemble our cadets. Some of them were on Governor's Island, some on Bedloe's Island in New York, others at Princeton, New Jersey, Yale University at New Haven, and in Illinois. But within a few days we managed to get the whole 150 together at Mineola. Meanwhile, Major McDill advised me about my uniforms and equipment, which I obtained.

Our contingent was certainly a hand-picked set of men. Every one of them was a college man and some were college graduates. Only a few of them had had any experience in flying. Most of the boys had their own cars, and the group took up quite a bit of parking space at Mineola. Among our cadets was Elliott Springs, who turned out to be one of the outstanding aces of the war, and who wrote several fascinating books about his flying experiences.

One day a smart-looking young gentleman appeared and reported for duty. He was apparently assigned to us because of his knowledge of Italian. He was eager to get into the service overseas and had joined us as a private rather than wait to receive a commission here. He was Albert

Spalding, one of America's greatest musicians. I had heard Spalding play the violin and was most happy that he was going to be with us. He got himself a tailor-made uniform which was the last word in what a soldier should wear. He played at a benefit concert in Carnegie Hall the night before we sailed and received a tremendous ovation. But later, in Italy, when he practiced his violin, the boys who wanted to be undisturbed at their poker used to suggest he go off where they couldn't hear him.

None of us knew much about Army paper work. We filled out the numerous forms in hit-or-miss fashion, figuring many of them never would be seen by anyone again. We had to establish our own mess, and I got orders to find a cook. No sooner said than done. I had a friend in Greenwich Village, Frank Giordano, who owned a small barber shop. I had gone there steadily since 1906 and was very fond of him. From the day war was declared I just could not get rid of Frank. He would be waiting for me at my apartment when I came to New York from Washington. He even came down to Washington to see me. He wanted to enlist in the Army. Everything was all right except that Frank was married, was over the age at which they were taking married men, had three children and flat feet. But what good was it having a friend in Congress, he wanted to know, if his friend couldn't even get him into the Army in wartime.

As soon as I got orders to find a cook, I thought of Frank. I arranged to get him the necessary waivers, and the first thing Frank knew he was in uniform and with our outfit. He was a mighty fine barber, but not much of a cook. Fortunately, that didn't make any difference while we were at Mineola, because all the boys ate in town, reported at the field after breakfast and went to town for lunch. We accumulated quite a lot of ration money which was put into our company fund, and Frank was very useful because he did a lot of barbering and ran errands for the boys at Mineola and on board ship.

One day Major McDill gave me a War Department order for 156 passages on any passenger liner sailing from the port of New York. We looked up the sailings and picked the Cunard Line's S.S. *Carmania*. McDill told me to go ahead and book the passages. I went down to the Cunard Line offices on lower Broadway, displayed my order and asked for 156 first-class passages. This was the first time the company had carried any aviation cadets, and the head of the passenger division was dubious about giving me first-class passages for them. I gave him all the arguments I could think of, but the only thing that really impressed him was my statement that I knew what I was talking about because I had helped shape the law that created such cadets. I told him I knew it was the intent of Congress that these cadets were entitled to first-class passage. (At least, I thought so.) At any rate, I got the 156 first-class tickets. Major McDill's eyes almost popped out when I showed him the big bunch of first-class passages. He remarked that if we got away with that, we were good, but he warned me that the responsibility was mine.

Well, this incident proved very interesting. It established a precedent, which was later approved by the Comptroller General of the United States. I am glad it was. Otherwise I would have been stuck for the difference between soldier rate—third-class or steerage—and first-class. I think the difference was about $150 a ticket. I would have been hard put to it to find $23,400.

But my troubles were just starting. Our detachment left Mineola by train and arrived at the pier in the Old Chelsea district of New York at six in the morning. Our boys soon took over the ship and were running all over the decks. Suddenly, a ship's officer came running around shouting, "Major in charge of aviation detachment, major in charge of aviation detachment." Major McDill responded and was told that the colonel in command of personnel wanted him to report to him at once. It was regulation for the senior commanding officer in rank on a ship carrying troops to act as commanding officer of all Army personnel aboard.

"For goodness' sake, La Guardia, I told you we would have trouble," Major McDill said. I went with him to see the commanding colonel. He was furious, and he ordered McDill to send our flying cadets down to steerage at once, since they were not yet commissioned officers. I insisted that they had the status of commissioned officers and were entitled to first-class passage. The colonel wanted to know what I had to do with it. I told him that I had obtained the tickets and that I had attended the initial conferences concerning our detachment. He was surprised and even more surprised when I told him that I had taken part in the discussions which created an Air Service when the aviation bill was up before Congress. In that way it came out that I was a member of Congress. Though the colonel was still fuming when the ship pulled out at the violation of the customs he had been used to in the Army, we managed to win the argument. We did have to send our "cook," Frank Giordano, Albert Spalding and a few clerks down to steerage.

When we landed in Liverpool, Major McDill received

orders to send the flying cadets who had been picked to go to Italy, to British flying schools instead and to report with me and our medical staff to headquarters in Paris. We were, of course, sorry to lose our men, for everyone had grown fond of one another in the time we had been together. Our cadets were trained in England and came out of the war with distinguished records; the casualties among them were also very high.

In Paris Major McDill and I learned that a cadet corps of 700 men was being formed there to go to Italy. About a hundred of them were already at the Italian training field at Foggia, an important aviation center in that war and which became an important aviation center again during World War II. It was my father's birthplace.

Before we left the United States I had been made a captain. Major McDill, our medical officers and I left Paris for Italy with 125 cadets in two railroad cars. These men, who had been detached from their original outfits to make up part of our group, I discovered, had received no pay and that no provision had been made for rations for them. In fact, they had already gone one full day without any food. I made arrangements for rations for our detachment at stations en route to Italy. We made the journey without too much hardship, though by no means in any luxury, for there were no sleeping accommodations on our troop train. At Foggia we reported to Major William Ord Ryan, a former West Point graduate, and a cavalry officer who later became a major general.

2

The United States government had arranged with the Italian government to give our flyers their preliminary military training and flying instruction in Italy. The Italian government agreed to provide instructors, housing and all flying equipment. We did not have sufficient flying instructors in the United States at that time to enable us to send any of them abroad, and we were greatly lacking in equipment. According to an estimate I made at the time, it cost the United States about $10,000 for each flying cadet from the time he began his first training until he got his wings.

The camp at Foggia was the best the Italians could do at the time, but it was not a completely equipped aviation center. Considering their limitations, the Italians made splendid efforts for the comfort and safety of our troops. Training and camp discipline were under the Italian command except for our troops, who were controlled by their own officers, so far as discipline was concerned.

The Italians had given us a splendid group of instructors, but, looking back at our experience today in the light of World War II, our methods of training seem so playful and childish and risky and dangerous. If a flyer was in the air for ten minutes at a time, that was considered quite a bit of training. With twelve or fifteen minutes in the air, the boy felt he had had a lucky break. Our training course started with the student racing a plane on the ground in a straightaway, grass-cut run. Then we learned to take off the ground, gain flying speed, attain an altitude of about twenty or thirty feet and then land again. After that came the usual circles, contra-circles and figure-eights. After a cadet had had as little as 120 to 180 minutes in the air he was permitted to make a solo flight.

The first solo flight was really the thrill that comes once in a lifetime. It was a great feeling, as the ship was first airborne, to realize that you were gaining altitude and were under your own control. It was exciting to make your first full circle of the field and come down again. The only one who suffered during that first solo flight was the instructor, who, watching from the ground, anxiously awaited your safe return. He could never tell whether we would land on the proper spot or even on the field at all. But the casualties in our preliminary training were very low. It was true then, and perhaps is true today, that the aptitude of a flyer could be pretty well determined by his first solo flight.

Very few of our boys had ever been off the ground before they got to Italy, and naturally they were all excited by their preliminary training. After it was completed, the cadets got their wings and their commissions. Classification of flyers as pilots, navigators and bombers was as primitive and crude as the training itself. The flyer's own preference was the deciding factor. We had no such thing as the careful screening for aptitudes given the flyers during World War II.

Our part of the training center at Foggia was divided into two camps, West Camp and South Camp. I was given command of West Camp. When Major Ryan, in command of the whole detachment, and I looked over the orders, we discovered that our cadets were supposed to get the rations of Italian enlisted men. These consisted of 2.20 pounds of dark black bread, issued in the morning, with a canteen of a black fluid substituting for coffee. The big meal of the day was at noon and consisted of a boiled macaroni paste or some other starch dish, a ladle of melted lard, and a handful of salt. Once a week there was a diminutive piece of boiled meat and some soup. Supper consisted of a bowl of gruel or vegetable soup and some more of the black fluid.

I could not see how we could keep Americans, used to our diet, healthy on that kind of food. Major Ryan and I talked the situation over and arranged to get our men fed temporarily at the Italian officers' mess. Before long, however, the full complement of 700 Americans would be occupying the post, and we could not continue this temporary arrangement. I suggested that we contract with a caterer to feed the men. We worked out a regular American breakfast, or as near to it as we could get under existing conditions. At mid-day we provided for a big, well-balanced meal, with a meat or fish course every day. We worked out a typical American supper. Major Ryan was rather doubtful about our authority to carry out this plan, but I told him that I thought we had to do it unless he could figure out any other way to get the men proper rations. It was I who signed the contract with the caterer.

After our rationing system had been functioning satisfactorily for several months, I was suddenly ordered by telegram to report to the Chief Quartermaster's office at Tours, France. I was instructed to bring along with me all data, records and the contract for feeding the cadets. I do not remember the name of the general I was to see, but he certainly was waiting for me.

After I was ushered into his office by his aide, Colonel Monnell, the general opened up on me right away. He stated that he was reporting the matter to the Judge Advocate General and charged me with violating the law, disregarding Army regulations, squandering public funds and acting generally like a convict, or something like that, rather than an officer and a gentleman. Then he pulled out papers and said the Italian government had paid the bills I had contracted and was now trying to collect the money from the American government under the master agreement between Italy and the United States for the training of cadets.

I explained to the general that it seemed a very simple matter to me. Then he tossed the Army regulations at me again.

"Is that all that is troubling you, General?" I asked. "If so, I can have all that changed very easily."

I thought the man would burst with rage. He pounded the desk violently, called me insolent, impertinent and demanded to know what I meant by saying that I could change Army regulations, which would take an act of Congress to accomplish.

"Well, I can get an act of Congress," I said.

Colonel Monnell burst out laughing. "General," he said, "you may as well admit that no one is going to be court-martialed for this thing. Mr. La Guardia knows what Congress would do if he returned and told them about it. Mr. La Guardia is a member of Congress."

You never saw a man change as fast as that general did when he heard that I was a Congressman. For the first time since I had come into the room, he asked me to be seated. I then explained in pretty straight language what our food situation was at Foggia. When he referred to Army regulations again and pointed out that some hardships were necessary, I stopped him and said that it was not a question of some hardships but one of either feeding the boys or practically starving them. He insisted that the Quartermaster's office could not pay for our catering because under his beloved Army regulations all troops had to be fed in accordance with regulations, either in organized messes for which there was specific allowance or on a specific per diem cash basis per man. I tried to get him to understand how impossible it would have been to turn our 700 men loose in a small community like Foggia to forage for themselves on a per diem allowance and pointed out that he knew as well as I did that no food was coming from the United States to Foggia to enable us to set up a regulation mess.

"Don't worry about having this bill paid," I suggested to the general. "I think it will be paid all right. I anticipated that we might have a little trouble, and I think I can fix that."

We parted as friends, and I went to Paris, where I talked the matter over in the office of the Air Service headquarters and presented the problem of financing to General Charles G. Dawes, who later became Vice President of the United States and was then chairman of the Interallied Finance Commission. He enjoyed a big laugh when he heard of my interview with the general in Tours. The whole matter was settled by General Dawes in less than three minutes; he arranged to have the Italian government present a separate bill for our food to the Interallied Finance Commission.

We had no disciplinary trouble at Foggia. Our camp was about five miles from the town, and the boys kept pretty busy. Our main source of irritation was the shortage of equipment which delayed our training schedules. Coming from the United States, where in 1917 we had so few military planes, we were impressed with the scores of Italian planes, though these cannot even be compared with the equipment in World War II for speed, striking power and destructiveness.

The United States had entered into an agreement with Italy in 1917 to buy a large number of planes. None of the orders had been fulfilled by the time we got to Italy. The United States had ordered about a thousand reconnaissance planes of a particular type. On paper it was the most beautiful design I had ever seen, and the plane was in production. These SIA's had been used on the Italian front for some time. A new type of SIA with increased speed and efficiency was the one on order for the United States. Though they were being turned out, I noticed a hesitancy about making deliveries. As we were frantic for equipment, we wondered why we were not getting delivery. I learned the real story. The new type was not satisfactory, and in several tests flyers had been killed. Italy did not want to deliver the planes to us until the government was sure of the plane. By inquiries in air circles we finally learned that the new plane was structurally weak.

Finally, deliveries of these new SIA's were made to us at Foggia, and large numbers of them were also delivered to our Air Force in Tours. Our experience with the plane proved no better than that of the Italians. We had a lieutenant of Marines attached to us at Foggia. How he ever got there none of us ever knew. Lieutenant Jordan was the first American to fly one of those SIA's; it buckled under him, and he was killed.

I kept the U.S. Air Service in Tours informed about the SIA planes. Then one day I informed the Italian factory making them that we did not care to receive any more of them at Foggia. I recommended to Tours that the order for them should be cancelled at once. Deliveries were held up, and trouble began for the Italian government. The SIA was a very powerful corporation. While the company recognized the weakness of the plane, it was anxious to get them off its hands. I argued vigorously with headquarters that American boys should not be required to fly those planes, and the contract was finally settled by agreement that the United States would take the planes on hand and cancel the rest of the order. The planes we received were not to be used in combat, but only for training purposes. Eugenio Chiesa, Italian Minister of Aviation, was quite put out about the cancellation of the order. He appealed to me to lay off the SIA, which, of course, I would not do.

Besides food and the quality of our equipment, another problem we had at Foggia was to safeguard the health of our personnel. Foggia was located in a malaria district. Dr. Oliver Kiel, a physician from Wichita Falls, Texas, established our own public health service there. The flat country provided no drainage, and the sewage system was primitive. Orders were issued to boil all drinking water, and instructions were drawn up for preparing raw vegetables. We scoured the countryside for screens. Each man's bunk was provided with a mosquito bar. We organized fly and mosquito detachments. The Italians thought we were crazy. We used what oil we could spare in mosquito and fly control projects. The result was that we had only one case of malaria in all the time we were at Foggia, much to the surprise of the Italians.

Dr. Kiel and I also worked out measures for prevention of venereal disease. We put out of bounds those places in the neighborhood where men could get infected. I gave a course of lectures on social disease and commercialized vice, while Dr. Kiel gave a course on prophylaxis. At

Christmas time 1917 we had a problem. The boys had accumulated leave and pay. There was nothing on which they could spend their money in Foggia. As our equipment was behind schedule, Christmas leave would not delay their training. We arranged for some of them to go to Rome, where we planned proper prophylactic arrangements. But we could not get accommodations for all of them in Rome, so some had to go to Naples, where we were unable to set up prophylactic stations because of lack of necessary personnel and supplies. Each man going to Naples gave his word that he would not expose himself to infection.

At the time Major Ryan was on special duty in France, and I was in command of the detachment. While we were in the midst of our medical precautions, Dr. Kiel came to my office and told me that Captain Sprague, our senior medical officer, was insisting that Army regulations did not permit supplies or personnel to be used as we were planning to use them. Soon afterwards Captain Sprague arrived at my office himself, with his written disapproval of our plans. As commanding officer, I wrote out an official order for the public health measures Captain Kiel and I had planned. Captain Sprague refused to carry them out, and I immediately placed him under arrest and appointed Captain Kiel acting medical officer. After the men had left for their leaves and our precautions had been put into effect, I released Sprague and restored him to his official duties. When the men returned from leave, results proved excellent.

Not long afterwards we received a formal order requesting that next time Captain La Guardia was at GHQ Chaumont, France, he report to headquarters of Surgeon General Merritt Ireland. I used to go to France at least once a month in the course of my duties. I came in for considerable ribbing about what was going to happen to me on my next trip, for the medical system Dr. Kiel and I had set up. By the time I got to General Ireland's headquarters at Chaumont, I wasn't sure that it was going to be a laughing matter.

I was a little relieved when General Ireland's aide courteously asked me to be seated. When the general came in, he greeted me cordially and said that the plan we had initiated for venereal disease control had been something they had been studying at GHQ; there had been discussions of it, and it had been tried out in some areas. He was very much interested in getting details of our experiment and a report on its results; and I was very much relieved. Then General Ireland asked my opinion on what duty Captain Sprague could best perform. I could not resist telling him that Captain Sprague was a stickler for paper work. "I think I can find a place for him," General Ireland replied. Sprague was transferred soon afterwards; I think into the Supply Corps.

My replacement for Captain Sprague was a big Swedish-American doctor from Minnesota. He worked cooperatively with us, except when he got drunk, when he wasn't good for anything. When I went back to France in 1919 with the delegation of the House Committee on Military Affairs for an inspection tour of our military installations, I ran into my medical replacement again. "Why don't you go home?" I asked him. "I can't go home," he replied. "This is a venereal disease center; I'm a prisoner here and can't go home until I am cured."

3

We had only been settled at Foggia a short time when the Battle of Caporetto began on the Italian front. The first big smash came on October twenty-fourth at two o'clock in the morning. It was terrific. Apparently, it had begun to dawn on the Germans that there might, after all, be an American Expeditionary Force. Therefore, they made their plans to break through in Italy, cut her off from her Allies by land, and run their western front right down to the Swiss border.

The Germans had spread alarming reports in Italy of the separate peace they were making with Russia. They planted information that German and Austrian troops were being transferred in great numbers from the Russian front to the Italian frontier. They predicted that Hindenburg would capture Rome. When the Austro-German drive actually began on the Italian front in October 1917, it was craftily headed with some German troops so that the Italians would the more readily believe that the huge numbers of German troops on the Russian front were about to be hurled against them. Some Italian regiments surrendered because of this fear and the feeling of hopelessness against such superior forces. This was some six or seven months before American troops could get into action in any numbers on the western front.

The fight at Caporetto was desperate, and Italy realized her great danger. Pleas were made to the Supreme Allied Command for reinforcements to be sent rapidly to Italy. Everybody was pressing for American troops, just a token representation at least.

The retreat to the Piave began on November fourth, and

the Italians up to that time had lost huge numbers in killed, wounded, missing and prisoners, as well as many heavy guns. General Diaz took over the command of the Italian Army from General Cadorna on November ninth. The Italian recovery on the Piave began that day. By November twenty-second the Italians had held their lines firm and were counter-attacking. British and French divisions which had been rushed to the front but held in reserve aided the Italians in December. The last Austro-German attack was repulsed on Christmas Day, turning a tide that threatened disaster for the whole Allied cause.

I had occasion to meet General Diaz. He gave me an oral message to take to General Pershing next time I was at American GHQ. He asked me to tell Pershing that the situation in Italy was desperate, that Diaz was badly in need of troop replacements, artillery, gas and such tanks as were then available. He pleaded particularly for American troops to bolster Italian morale. I reported all this to General Pershing. On going into his office to see Pershing, I was a little nervous. But my task was easier than I had anticipated, and he soon made me feel at ease. He brought out the whole story by his few direct questions. Then he told me of the demands upon him for American troops from all sides. He said that I might as well make it clear to the Italians that there would be no token representation of American troops; that our troops would fight as a unit, and not until we had a front of our own and were in condition to occupy it. General Pershing thought the kind of detachment we had of American aviators in Italy was a good thing, because it not only supplemented the Italian air force but gave our men valuable training on this active front.

There can be no doubt that Caporetto caused panic in Italy. Francesco Nitti, whom I had met when he was in Washington with the Italian mission soon after our declaration of war, was Minister of Finance. He was, perhaps, the most powerful member of the Italian Cabinet. He told me that there was hardly a neutral nation in the world that had not sent Italy peace feelers. He said that within the Cabinet there was a strong feeling that a separate peace might be necessary. I informed our military authorities of these conversations, though the facts were undoubtedly well known to them. However, after the tide had turned, Italy began to snap back pretty fast and showed tremendous stamina and determination to carry on.

In November 1917, while the Battle of Caporetto was still raging, I was on one of my trips to Paris. I reported to our headquarters and to the American public in an interview that while the situation in Italy was undoubtedly grave, I was optimistic and believed it was far from hopeless. Grumbling was plentiful in Italy at that time, particularly because of the lack of decent food for civilians and sufficient supplies for the war effort. Butter was almost impossible to get; bread was black and soggy and tasteless; meat scarce; coal and steel for making munitions were lacking; and there was such a shortage of shipping in the Allied world that sufficient supplies could not be sent to Italy from the United States, Great Britain and France.

One afternoon I was ordered back to Foggia on short notice because of the grave situation in Italy. My only instructions were that if we were cut off by the Germans we must use our heads and do the best we could. When I returned, I soon went up to the front. I shall never forget that day when I took our first detachment of American flyers to the Italian front to report for duty with the Italian Army. There were twenty-four of us. But before long we had a few hundred American flyers on that front. The Italian High Command gave the first batch of us a luncheon in Padua. The chief officer, in extending a welcome to us, said in the usual complimentary manner, I suppose, that if there was anything we wanted, all we had to do was to ask for it. I told him that was easy; I wanted to ask for something right there and then: we wanted to go on a mission the following morning. The request was granted.

Our duty missions were not to be compared with missions in World War II. Our boys were divided among some ten Italian squadrons, stationed at Padua, Verona and Aquila. Our cruising radius was not more than a couple of hundred miles at most. Since the Austrians were well within Italian territory, we had to be careful not to bomb our own people. Bombing was not popular in the Italian war zone then; the population felt that if we did not go out on bombing raids, the Austrians would not come and bomb them in return.

Our objectives were principally air fields, munition dumps, freight centers. We were careful never to drop any bombs over a city, and every mission was confined to a very small target. All of our bombing planes were tri-motor Capronis, as efficient a plane as any then built. Though we had three motors, their total horsepower was only 450. In World War II our B-29 four-motor planes had between 2,200 and 2,400 horsepower. Loaded, we flew at about 110 miles an hour and coming back could manage between 115 and 120. At times we were well protected by Italian, French and British pursuit planes. The German and Austrian anti-aircraft defense, though sometimes accurate, was not nearly so deadly as anti-aircraft fire is now. Before long our pilots did not have much respect for it or fear of it. On the whole our missions were rather a tame job. They seemed exciting enough at the time, but their glamour has been dimmed by the nature of such things in World War II.

My companions in the Italian squadron with which I went on air raids were Major Piero Negrotto, a member of the Italian Parliament, Captain Fred Zoppoloni, Italian ace bomber, and a rear gunner named Fumani. We worked in the Piave district and made day and night forays into Austria. I was the left-hand pilot in this plane and also acted as bombardier.

Before joining the air service, Major Negrotto had been in the trenches in the Asiago district. We were flying over that sector one day and on our return from a bombing mission. Major Negrotto suddenly decided he would like to take a look at his old trenches and strafe the enemy, now in possession of them, with his machine gun. He swooped down, and while we were thus engaged, we got separated from our escort. When we ascended higher again to head for home, two Austrian planes attacked us. Things were getting rather hot, and our Caproni had quite a few holes in it, when some English planes came to our rescue, shot down one of the Austrians and drove the other away. One night when we were returning from a raid, we were caught in a cross-light system of searchlights and were in the middle of a well-directed barrage of anti-aircraft fire. The searchlight was on us for at least four minutes. Our machine was riddled with holes before we got back to our own camp. None of us was hurt. Whenever we passed through an enemy barrage, Major Negrotto would take off his flying goggles and put on his monocle to show his indifference.

I was surprised one day while I was at the front to receive a telegram from Colonel M. C. Buckey, our military attaché in Italy, asking me to come to Rome. Colonel Buckey had been a cavalry officer. His job was to keep Washington informed about what was going on in Italy, and he hated being out of action at the front.

When I got to Rome, Colonel Buckey took me to see our Ambassador to Italy, Thomas Nelson Page, a scholarly novelist, and a fine type of American gentleman. Colonel Buckey and the Ambassador were both very much worried about the anti-American propaganda with which the Germans were filling Italy. They were determined to fight back at it, and Coloney Buckey thought it would be a good idea, since I knew Italian, if I made a series of speeches in big cities in Italy. I said that I was willing to do it, if they thought it would do any good. The Ambassador said that the feeling toward the United States was not good because the Italian people had not yet had visible evidence of American participation in the war, though their leaders knew the part we were playing.

A public meeting had been arranged in the Stock Exchange at Genoa. If that was successful, Ambassador Page and Colonel Buckey planned a series of such meetings in key cities. Ambassador Page told me that I must understand that if the meeting in Genoa did not go well, and if my talk was not well received, that he would have to repudiate me and state publicly that I was not talking for the American government. He would have to deny any reports that he had had anything to do with the meeting. If, on the other hand, I was well received, he would stand back of me and accept sponsorship of this and the other meetings. I was a bit taken aback, but I thought the importance of the project was worth the risk. Then Ambassador Page threw one at me that I did not like so much. He said that if any bitterness was created as a result of my talk in Genoa, he might have to ask the Army to withdraw me from Italy. I was afraid of running the risk of being sent home altogether, but Ambassador Page thought he could protect me so far as that might be concerned.

I hot-footed it to Genoa, and I spoke to a huge crowd there on the part the United States was playing in the war. Luckily for me they were very enthusiastic. Thereafter I addressed huge mass meetings in Rome, Milan, Naples, Bologna, Turin, Florence and Bari. I discussed American motives and intentions, which the Germans branded as selfish greed and a predatory effort to protect our money loaned to the Allies. The Germans were also telling the Italians that we had entered the war to prolong it, while I stressed that we had entered it to finish it. I carefully explained in simple terms President Wilson's peace aims, discussed the purposes for which we were fighting, outlined our food and fuel policies and appealed passionately for full support by Italians of their war loans. Warm demonstrations occurred in favor of the United States at all these meetings, and the Ambassador never had to repudiate me.

These missions were rather hard on me. They always entailed traveling two nights in order not to lose more than one day at our camp or at the front. My service at the front seemed my most peaceful activity since I had landed in Italy.

After I had returned to active duty from one of my

morale speeches, I went on a raid with my Italian team one day to bomb an Austrian aviation camp. When we arrived over the camp, I dropped my bomb. Before I had time to find out whether I had scored a hit, Captain Zoppoloni made a sharp turn to the right. I asked him what the result had been, and Zoppoloni throttled down the motors right over the barrage being sent up against us and shouted, "It was the best speech you ever made."

4

During our service on the Italian front, King Victor Emmanuel III came to Padua to spend the day. After a General Staff luncheon, the King awarded decorations to all branches of the service. I was very proud of the six American flyers who were awarded the Flying Cross of Italy. I was somewhat embarrassed, however, when it turned out that the Italian authorities had allotted seven awards for American flyers. This caused them some embarrassment too, so they handed me the seventh cross. The King was very cordial when he pinned the cross on me and held me in conversation longer than usual, apparently because the error had attracted some attention.

Later, I received an invitation to dine with the King. I took Albert Spalding along with me. He had now got a commission as lieutenant and I was happy that he was assigned to our detachment in Italy, where he became our adjutant. On the way to the King's headquarters we expected to be briefed on etiquette, but His Majesty's military aide and the other officers who accompanied us limited the briefing to a simple statement that since the country was at war the usual formalities in peacetime would be dispensed with.

The King and his staff were occupying a striking-looking building, right up in the front zone, which I believe had been a monastery. Soon after our reception by the King's chancellor and other members of his personal staff, Victor Emmanuel entered. He came up to me and addressed me cordially, welcomed me to his temporary home and hoped that the day would soon come when I could visit him and his family at their real home in Rome. The King asked me many questions about America in rather rapid-fire order, indicating to me that he knew about conditions and had not just been briefed at the last moment on particular subjects. By the time we sat down to dinner with ten or twelve of the King's staff, we were conversing easily in both Italian and English, which the King knew well.

I told the King of my meeting with Major Gabriele d'Annunzio. I had told d'Annunzio that he and I had a great deal in common. He had stiffened and asked what I meant. "You are in the Air Service, so am I," I answered. "You make speeches; I make speeches too. The people don't understand your Italian, but they pretend they do. They don't understand me either, but they ask what I am trying to say." The King thought it very funny, but d'Annunzio didn't.

After dinner, the King beckoned to me to join him in front of the fireplace. We talked of Italy's position in the war. One could see that Victor Emmanuel hated war and was proud that his country could never be listed as a warmonger. He construed the Triple Alliance with Germany and Austria as purely defensive and was opposed to Italy's joining those two countries when they attacked in 1914.

He wondered whether the outside world fully appreciated the position Italy had taken at that time. He felt it could not have taken any other course.

We also discussed the difficulties of modern warfare and its terrible destruction and enormous cost. We got to talking about shortage of ships, and I told the King of reports I had read on the slow operations at Genoa and other Italian ports, where the turn-around time for ships was too long. "Yes, I have heard of that too," the King said. "But you should take that up with Signor Nitti in Rome. You see, I am not the President of a republic. I am only a king. I have not many powers."

That brought up the subject of dynasties, and I expressed my belief that the days of monarchies were numbered. The King concurred. Neither of us, however, foresaw the intervening period of dictatorships. Toward the close of our talk that night the King said something that made a deep impression on me. "Of course, war must be ended," he said. "War can end if we give the peoples of the world an opportunity to live decently. In the meantime, there may be many experiments in government. I, for one, am trying to give my son an education. I would never risk the life of one doughboy to protect my throne or that of my son."

A few years later when a small group of loud-mouthed Fascists moved on Rome and Badoglio asked for one battalion of troops to chase them out, King Victor Emmanuel III refused to protect his throne from them. That was the end of Victor Emmanuel III and the beginning of Mussolini.

I really do not remember whether I met Benito Mussolini during my visit to Milan during the war. He was in some government office there, having served his time at the front and been wounded. In many small Italian communities the Fascisti were vocal even at that time. I met several delegations of them the day I made my first appearance at La Scala and later ran into some others at a bombing school.

The younger element in Italy was most restive. They wanted to bring about a change in their world. They were not at all satisfied with the monarchy. The form of government, however, was not the real issue. That issue was how much say the people were to have in the conduct of the affairs of government. The cost of living, public education and public health were all vital problems in Italy during the war, and they were the subjects of intense discussion among the younger element.

I was convinced that a big change was coming in Italy. In fact, a big change did come to Italy, but hardly what I expected. Instead of more democracy, Italy was deprived of the democratic forms she had developed. Economic conditions, at best, during my observations there, were bad. Great inequalities existed. The tax system was unfair. Special privilege was very much in the saddle, just as it has been in our own country at various periods.

I used to talk over the situation at length with Francesco Nitti, who had a very clear mind and who considered these basic problems facing his country with a great deal of understanding. He was also practical and realistic. He felt that conditions in Italy would not improve at the rate of reform required, and that therefore there would have to be fundamental changes. After Italy had gone through a difficult period, Nitti was confident and hopeful about the future of his country. Most students of affairs in Italy during the first world war felt, I believe, that a transition period involving something close to communism, might well follow the war. They felt, however, that the temper of the Italian people being what it was, the stern discipline required by the Communist system would not be accepted. Italy, in their opinion, would develop into a representative republic with an economy close to state socialism.

It looks now as if we were, after two wars and a period of dictatorship, in about the same fundamental position as after World War I, with none of the basic problems settled in any country. It is universally accepted that war is not a solution, that a better distribution of the good things of life must be brought about. But the old, selfish interests continue to resist change and betterment. The inequalities in the distribution of raw materials, excess food supplies and other commodities, which have caused war after war, still exist. Though documents such as the Atlantic Charter and other official statements recognize these problems and offer hope, very little, if any, real progress in the way of actual remedies has been made.

5

In the middle of March 1918 I was due in Paris for one of the monthly conferences I attended at Air Service headquarters. I was scheduled to make a two-and-a-half hour cross-country test flight, and I was anxious to get that over with and go to Paris. I had exercised all the authority I could to get the Chief Flying Officer to consent to let me take off, though it was a nasty, windy day. The course was triangular. On the last leg of it I ran into serious trouble. The wind had greater speed than the forward speed of my plane. Soon my plane was completely out of control. It kicked around and fussed around, and there seemed nothing I could do. I had a map as a gasoline guide, and I soon found from it that I was several miles out of my course and beyond the limits on my map. I cruised around, and went down low, trying to get my location by looking for something that seemed like a military installation. I must have suddenly run into an unusually strong gust of wind, which overturned my plane. Fortunately my safety belt broke as I crashed, and that saved me from being crushed under the motor. After all, I was not able to leave for Paris that night. My injuries consisted of some contusions on the left hip, but after a short stay in hospital, I was able to get back to flying duty and was in Paris by April fourth.

By the spring of 1918 shipping had become such a critical problem that Italy was very short of supplies. Frantic efforts had to be made to enable her to fulfill her commitments to the United States for trucks, automobiles, airplane motors and airplanes. The Italian government had a contract with Spain for delivery of several thousand tons of steel. The lira, however, had depreciated, and there was danger that Italy would not be able to carry out this contract for vitally needed steel. The Italians suggested that the United States take over the contract and get the steel to Italy, thus saving tonnage from the United States. It seemed a simple enough arrangement, but there was some hitch in getting that steel out of Spain.

In Paris I was told to go to Spain and make the necessary arrangements for the transfer of the steel contract from the Italian to the American government. Germany was bringing great pressure on Spain at the time to stop deliveries to Italy. I decided to take Lieutenant Albert Spalding with me to Spain. Our first job was to get some civilian clothes in Paris. He was easy to fit, for he wore all his clothes well, but we had considerable trouble fitting me in Paris stores.

Our Spanish mission was not difficult. The mill-owners were most friendly, and the British Intelligence had the situation well in hand. They seemed always to be able to keep one export permit ahead. Spain was not prosperous at the time and was willing to sell anything it had to anybody who could pay for it.

The country was largely pro-German. While I was in Barcelona, I was interviewed by *La Publicidad*. I told the Spanish people that they were injuring themselves by their friendliness toward Germany. I pointed out that German submarines were sinking Spanish ships carrying raw materials vitally needed in Spain. The Germans in their propaganda in Spain were harping on the Spanish-American War. I pointed out that the Germans had sunk seventy-eight Spanish merchant ships of a total tonnage of over 160,000 and that Spain's factories could not continue to operate unless they got raw materials from the United State. I told them that our victory meant their prosperity, but that a German victory meant domination and exploitation of Spain in the interests of Germany.

I think it was the second morning that I was in Madrid that I was approached while I was being shaved in a barber shop by a tall, heavy-set Negro. He said he wanted to talk to me and asked if I was a Congressman. I looked at him more closely, and his appearance seemed familiar. Then one of the staff of the American Embassy stepped up to me and said that the Negro was Jack Johnson, former heavyweight champion of the world. The Embassy man had suggested he talk to me. Johnson was under indictment in Illinois on a white slavery charge. He had jumped bail and landed up in Madrid after barnstorming in Europe. Now, with the war on, he could not get out of Spain. He told me his long story and claimed he had been persecuted in Chicago. He wanted me to help him get into the American Army. I told him to write out his whole story and state that he would accept service anywhere and perform any duty assigned to him. All I could do, I warned him, was to get it into the hands of the proper military authorities.

Next day I got this letter from Jack Johnson:

"After my talk with you yesterday, it occurred to me to ask you to use your good offices in my behalf. I am as good an American as any one living and naturally I want to do my bit. I firmly believe I wasn't fairly treated at home.

"All I ask now is a chance to show my sincerity. America is my country.

"There's no position you could get for me that I would consider too rough or too dangerous. I am willing to fight and die for my own country. I cannot offer any more."

I referred Johnson's offer to the Adjutant General, making it clear that I did not know anything about his trouble in Illinois. I added that I believed it would be hard to deprive any American of the right to fight. But Jack Johnson was turned down by both the Army and the Navy.

While I was in Spain in June 1918, I met a very interesting gentleman, Commander Crowley, who had recently come out of Russia, where the Bolsheviks had come into power only eight months before. Commander Crowley had been our naval attaché in Petrograd and was withdrawn and sent to Spain as our naval attaché. He told me of the mistakes we and the British were making in our intervention in the internal affairs of Russia. In Milan I had had the opportunity of getting a similar viewpoint from North Winship, formerly American Consul General at Petrograd, who had been recalled from Russia at the request of our Ambassador, David R. Francis, because he was critical of the counter-revolutionary activities the Allies were carrying on there.

When I got back to Paris from Spain, I had a talk with Franklin Bouillon, who held the rank of minister in the French government. He was a very discouraged man. He felt that the situation was extremely critical, and that unless the United States threw terrific forces into action in a very short time, the Allies could no longer hold out. Speaking to me as one member of a parliament to another, M. Bouillon told me that he thought I could best serve the cause by going back to the United States and letting our government know how critical the situation was and how much more must be done by the United States to meet it. I listened attentively, but I did not tell M. Bouillon that I would not think of going home to tell our people that the war was being lost. I told M. Bouillon that I thought perhaps he did not realize all that was being done by the United States and suggested that things would improve once we got into action in any numbers on the front.

This conversation took place at a dinner party to which two other members of the French parliament had been invited as well as Whitney Warren, the American architect. During the conversation an amusing coincidence occurred —at least it seemed funny to me at the time. M. Bouillon was in the midst of quite an impassioned plea to me. "Our beloved Paris is being bombed," he said emotionally. At

that moment we heard the terrific noise of a bomb falling.
M. Bouillon went right on talking, merely adding in tones
of an advocate emphasizing his evidence: *"Voila!"*

When I got back to Italy, I checked Bouillon's pessi-
mism with Nitti. I did not tell him Bouillon's views, but
I asked him for a frank statement of his opinion of the
situation.

"Well, I will tell you," Nitti said. "We are all praying
for the best. We are all discouraged. I realize that there is
no need for being so discouraged, because what your country has already done has been miraculous. Yet, the fact
remains that here it is May, going on June, and we have
been pushed back and pushed back. We have had not one
large, impressive, successful offensive. I am watching
Clemenceau; Clemenceau is watching Lloyd George;
Lloyd George is watching me. Every one of us is scared
to death that it will be one or the other who will first
broach the subject of peace."

I was startled by the grave view these men who were in
positions to be best informed took of the situation. But
I did not lose confidence that General Pershing would put
American troops into action in time and strike hard when
he was ready and not before. I felt sure that when he did
strike, he would do the job assigned to him. And that is
what he did do a few weeks later at Château-Thierry. After that successful battle, the atmosphere in Italy visibly
improved. I am happy now, as I look back on those trying
days, that I merely listened patiently to these notes of despair but made no official communication of them to Congress or the people, as I was urged to do.

The tide began definitely to turn in favor of the Allies
in June 1918, and there was never again any loss of confi-

dence in victory. During the rest of the summer, the Germans were steadily driven back by the combined force of the French, British, Italian and American troops.

On August 5, 1918, I was promoted to the rank of major, a title some of my friends used for me for many years afterwards. After it looked certain that the German collapse was only a matter of weeks, I was ordered home, on some military planning mission, which finally proved unnecessary because of the impending victory. Meanwhile, the Congressional elections of 1918 were very near, and I arrived in New York on October twenty-eighth in time to take part in the tag end of the campaign for my re-election.

CHAPTER VIII

Back in the Fray

1

THE CAMPAIGN for renomination and re-election to Congress had begun in July 1918. While I was busy on the Italian front, petitions had been circulated in my 14th Congressional District by pacifists asking that my seat be declared vacant and a special election to replace me be held in the district. The Women's Peace Party, of 70 Fifth Avenue, one of the most powerful peace organizations in the country, had its headquarters within my district, and it was very active in circulating petitions declaring that it was unconstitutional for me to be in the Army and retain my seat in Congress. One of the leaders of this movement was a charming lady for whom I always had great regard, Mrs. Philip Lydig, who afterwards became the wife of the Reverend Percy Stickney Grant, pastor of the Church of the Ascension, whom I was always proud to call a friend.

The slogan of the movement to unseat me was "Let's be Represented," and quite a few signatures appeared on the petition. While I was abroad, I had cast the deciding vote for the woman suffrage amendment. The Women's Peace Party planned to run a woman for my seat. Sam Koenig, Republican leader, sent a message to Speaker Clark: "No Congressman should be punished for enlisting in war service." Speaker Clark told me after I got back to the United

States that he had put the petitions in his drawer. "If anything happens to La Guardia," he told the committee which visited him, "the question will be academic. It will be time enough then to see what we can do about it." He also told the petitioners that he did not have the power to declare my seat vacant.

The Buffalo *Enquirer* remarked: "Congressman La Guardia, absent to fight for his country, is absent little more than some Congressmen during the baseball season. Why raise a fuss over him?" In Rome a New York *Times* correspondent showed me a dispatch about the petitions to unseat me and asked for my comment. I told him: "I am now working not only for my district, but for my country. You might say that if any signers of the petition will take my seat in a Caproni biplane, I shall be glad to resume my upholstered seat in the House."

Meanwhile, a movement had been started in the United States by the National Security League and other groups to nominate patriotic Congressmen by both the Democrats and the Republicans in New York. On July 30, 1918, the executive committee of the Republican and Democratic parties in New York County agreed on fusion nominations including mine.

These committees were determined to defeat any Socialist candidates, and particularly Meyer London, who represented the 12th New York District, and Morris Hillquit, who was seeking the nomination in the 20th District. In my district the Socialists named Scott Nearing on a platform calling for an early negotiated peace. He was under indictment at the time for interference with the prosecution of the war. My supporters contrasted my war record and played up my decorations, the Italian War Cross, the

Merit of War and Knight of the Crown, and they also stressed my record on labor unions and my activities with them.

When I arrived back in New York in October and went to the Hotel Brevoort, reporters flocked to interview me and told me that Scott Nearing's indictment was based on the publication and circulation of a pamphlet by the American Socialist Society called "The Great Madness," which attacked the draft law and the Liberty Loans. I told the reporters that I did not even know what my opponent looked like and therefore could not comment on him. I pointed out that there were plenty of Socialists in England, France, Italy and Germany who were fighting for their countries, but I added this note of caution: "The question of patriotism must not be introduced into this campaign. Scott Nearing must have a fighting chance. I did not know that he was under indictment, but remember this—under the laws of this country a man is innocent until he is proved guilty."

The results in the Congressional elections, since bipartisan nominations had been made, were a foregone conclusion. But otherwise the campaign was a lively one. Al Smith was running for Governor that year against Charles S. Whitman, who was up for re-election. The night after my arrival in New York, I went to a political meeting at the Lenox Assembly Rooms in Second Street, at which Governor Whitman was the speaker. The crowd gave me an enthusiastic reception when they caught sight of me, so I wasn't worried about my re-election.

I was anxious to get back to work in the House of Representatives. I did not wait for the regular process of demobilization to take its long course. I simply sent in my resignation to the President, and after it was acknowledged and accepted by the War Department, I got the old suit out of camphor and returned to the House.

As election day drew near, I agreed to debate with my opponent, Scott Nearing, in Cooper Union. The debate was courteous. When it came my turn to speak, I said:

"The issue in the 14th Congressional District is the same as the issue on the Western and Austrian front. I am personally opposed to militarism, imperialism and all manner of oppression. I am against war, and because I am against war I went to war to fight against war. I don't think we can end war by merely talking against war on the corners of the East Side." I claimed that socialism had proved itself a failure in Russia, and that the refusal of the German Socialists to protest against the butchery by German militarists was another outstanding instance of its failure in a crisis. I maintained that I had been doing for the people of my district and my country, while a member of the House, the very things the Socialists claimed they could do if elected. When Nearing attacked profiteers, for instance, I pointed out that I had introduced a bill providing the death penalty for them in wartime. In closing, I said that I had been told that my opponent was a professor of economics. "It's a mistake," I said, "he's a poet."

2

When I got back to the House, I certainly found the profiteers buzzing around the capital. The liquidation of our huge war supplies was a great opportunity for profiteering, and great care had to be taken to protect the interests of the people. The people themselves were sick of the war, tired of hearing about it, and in no mood to face their responsibilities for post-war reconstruction of the devastated countries and their disrupted economies. Not enough Americans realized the great significance of those problems. The public wanted to forget Europe, forget war and ignore the problem of preventing future wars. The result was that Europe was to become once more a fertile breeding ground for world war.

The lack of information in this country on European politics, even as late as Armistice Day 1918, was astounding. The indifference to Europe and the world situation in general was noticeable everywhere. There was great rejoicing over the Allied victory. There was acceptance of the fact that we had rendered a useful service to humanity in stepping in and preventing the military autocracies of the Hohenzollerns and the Hapsburgs from controlling the world. There the American people seemed satisfied to place a period. "Now let's get the boys home; let's mind our own business from now on," was the attitude. We were going to have no more wars. We would cut our budget and reduce taxes. We did not feel we needed any large military establishment. There was a tendency to believe that the agricultural interests had had too much to say during the war and must be deflated in favor of the manufacturing and financial interests. There seemed no limit to our resources. Now seemed the time for big investments with our surplus capital. Efficiency in industry was said to be promoted by big mergers of big companies. We must keep America clean by kicking out all Socialists and leaving no place for foreign "isms" in American life. These slogans of the day were not all written down in any one list. Each item was given careful consideration, however, by some special interests and eventually they were all carried out—all summing up to disaster for our country.

The Republicans had carried Congress in the November 1918 elections. This was attributed to President Wilson's political blunder in appealing to the people to elect a Democratic majority. I do not believe that was the real cause. The Republicans played up the President's appeal during the campaign and characterized it as ingratitude for the support they had given the administration during the war. I think the election results, rather, reflected the desire for a change and were more the result of the accumulation of gripes and kicks that war always brings than they were the result of the President's appeal. In the Senate the Republicans won 48 seats to the Democrats' 46, and in the House the Republicans won 239 to 190 for the Democrats. There were a few members of miscellaneous parties.

While he was in Paris at the Peace Conference, President Wilson sent a call for a special session of Congress to meet on May 19, 1919. New appropriation bills were required before July first. The War Risk Insurance Bureau had to be refinanced. Taxes, the tariff, repeal of wartime prohibition, and labor legislation were some of the measures mentioned in President Wilson's message to Congress. He also stressed the great importance of aid for returned soldiers to get jobs. The end of hostilities in Europe did not find the War Department as well prepared for the return of our troops from overseas as it was after World War II, though the task was many times greater after that second war.

There had been no planning for the cancellation of war contracts, and a bill granting authority to settle or compromise these contracts and claims had to be hurriedly thrown together and passed. The Bureau of Supplies of the War Department intended to turn over Army surplus copper to the copper interests on terms that gave them fees they were not entitled to and enabled them to keep up the price of copper beyond what it should have been. The copper people were even to get fees for selling the government's copper to themselves. I brought out this scandal into the open on the floor of the House.

The Army had millions of cans of corned beef and roast beef and millions of pounds of bacon in its warehouses after the war. The head of the Bureau of Surplus Supplies asked the advice of the packers, who had sold these supplies to the government at a good profit, about what he should do with them. They told him, among other things, that the American people could not eat the bacon the government had paid good money for to feed its soldiers. I had eaten it often in Europe, and I was able to testify that it was excellent bacon. But the packers told their friend in the Surplus Supplies Bureau that it would have to be recured. The director of that bureau also testified that he could not sell six-pound cans of corned beef and roast beef because no family in this country could use six pounds at a time. "Evidently the corps of experts are not familiar with vital statistics or appetites of families," I suggested to the House. When we asked in committee hearings what the director was going to do with all that good food, he said vaguely that he thought he might find a market for it in Rumania or Bosnia or Herzegovina! I pointed out that those countries never had used canned beef and, in fact, used very little meat at all. I also maintained that you could not find a can opener in all of Rumania in 1919.

The head of the Bureau of Supplies, who got $25,000 a

year from the government and had formerly been an executive of the U.S. Gas & Improvement Company, had sent out circulars to the Salvation Army offering this surplus meat. I reminded the House that the Salvation Army specialized in doughnuts and not in bacon. It surprised me, I told my colleagues, that he had not offered that bacon to some Jewish synagogues. I suggested that if he would put that bacon and corned beef and roast beef on the open market in New York or Philadephia or Boston, he would soon find enough hungry people willing to buy it and eat it. But that would have helped to bring down the high cost of living, which the packers who were advising the director of the Bureau of Surplus Supplies were helping to keep up by their exorbitant price demands for their meat.

One of the most disgraceful deals in surplus supplies was the transaction whereby the Army disposed of airplanes it had purchased from the Curtiss Company for $22,631,200 to the same company for $2,700,000. The Curtiss Company even had the nerve to serve notice that it would sue the government if it tried to sell those planes to anybody else. These planes were not junk. They were flown from the fields by the Curtiss people after their purchase, as I pointed out to the House.

The head of the Bureau of Post Exchanges of the Army was asking for authority to spend $1,000,000 to buy the buildings erected by the Red Cross and the Y.M.C.A. at Army cantonments. These buildings had been gifts of the American people, who had raised the money for the Red Cross and Y.M.C.A. They already belonged to the government. We managed to cut the Bureau of Post Exchange appropriation from its requested $5,875,000 to $150,000.

3

In 1919 I was proud of my role in reducing the Army of the United States. I know now what a mistake I made. I find that I said in the House on August 28, 1919: "I think the best thing I ever did in my short legislative life was in opposition to the appropriation bill in which we cut down the Army from 507,000 to an average of 300,000." But I went through another world war, and after it was over, I wrote an article which was published in *The Reader's Digest* for April 1947 entitled "Why I *Now* Believe in Universal Military Training."

In that article * I confessed that I had helped my country to make one of the most serious mistakes in its history. As we were in danger of repeating the same tragic blunder, I wanted to confess. Secretary of War Newton D. Baker had come before the House Military Affairs Committee in 1919 and had asked for a peacetime army of a million men, half to be enlisted voluntarily, half to be conscripted. Shocking! Why on earth was Mr. Baker asking for such extreme action?

Secretary Baker explained that our responsibilities under the Peace of Versailles would be grave, and greatest of all would be our obligation to see that peace was maintained. He said unless we did our full share—and that included backing up our policy with strong armament—we, the members of the Military Affairs Committee, would live to see another—and far more terrible—world war.

Could anything sound more preposterous? So we persuaded ourselves! Had we not just overthrown the military autocracies of the Hohenzollerns and the Hapsburgs? Was

* Quoted in part herein by permission of *The Reader's Digest.*

not Japan our ally? China weak? And certainly Russia could never again form an army. Great Britain, France and Italy would look after the peace of Europe. Why should we get into it? The idea of maintaining armies to keep the peace in Europe and the Far East was madness. There would be no more wars. We would stay home and mind our business!

Our committee took a long look at the War Department's request for funds to train 500,000 men under compulsory training—and chucked it out. But I had still not done my worst. In its final report, our committee did leave in provision for 500,000 soldiers by voluntary enlistment. But I announced that I would fight the plan on the floor of the House and seek to reduce the size of the Army. To my surprise, many of my colleagues agreed to help me against the plans of the War Department. I made a motion in the House to reduce the Army by 200,000. It carried easily. The next year the Army was still further reduced. The rest is history.

All our young men now deserve something better than our present dangerously unsatisfactory peacetime military policy. What we have is an enormously expensive army which is becoming more inefficient in reverse ratio to its increased cost. Worse, it is becoming more and more a strictly professional army. Naturally, well-paid and experienced commissioned and noncommissioned personnel are necessary for any army—but that is not enough.

This time the American people must not be allowed to overlook the fact that the new peace brings frightful new responsibilities. There might have been some excuse twenty-eight years ago, for really we did not know any better. It was all so new to us. We made that mistake once, and it may truthfully be said that we paid very highly for it. We have a great deal more experience now.

I see a tendency already to refuse sufficient men for the military establishment; reluctance fully to assume the costly responsibilities of peace. Indeed, I see a certain timidity, even on the part of the War Department, as well as the administration, in presenting to Congress clearly and forcefully all the facts that make peacetime training necessary. Even the latest recommendation of a six months' training period is ineffective; it's wrong and everybody in the War Department knows it. It's not enough.

I advocate a system of universal, national training that will exempt no one. But why such drastic steps for preparedness, the skeptic asks. In the same words, the same tone of voice that I used back in 1919, he demands to know:

"Who is getting ready to fight us? Who is going to start trouble again? Who wants another war? Who?"

God knows; I do not. That is why I speak so bluntly now, while there is still time to avoid another war. We dare not ignore the present world situation. No man can predict the groupings of nations, friendly or antagonistic, should the world be cursed with another conflict. None of us wants war, but do you know anyone who can give us an assurance that it will not come again?

Many of us are devoting all of our efforts to bring about a better understanding among the peoples of the world. But in a frightfully realistic lesson I have learned that to advocate preparedness is not at all incompatible with a consuming desire for peace.

If skeptics challenge the meaning I draw from bitter experience, I must say to them (speaking entirely from hindsight, which is always easy) that had we followed Secretary Baker's service plans, which I helped to kill, and Woodrow Wilson's peace plans, which others destroyed, Hitler would never have dared to move beyond his boundaries. It is a fact that when the Italian sanctions were proclaimed by the League of Nations, Great Britain was not in a position to enforce them. They were not prepared. Mussolini and Hitler knew that. This statement is not conjecture on my part. Anthony Eden told me so. Such helplessness in the face of a crisis was the start of Hitler's war of aggression. Knowing Britain was not ready, he also believed we could not prepare in time to help her.

My old friend General Billy Mitchell used to say that no country ever strikes at another until its military leaders believe they can win. That is why it will be a good thing if we, who do not want war, make ourselves invincible. An essential part of that program will be universal training. In addition to its benefits to the nation as a whole, and to young men as individuals, it will keep recalcitrant nations in line—for no one would go to war to lose.

Again the skeptic will urge that I propose universal military training while the nations are making plans to disarm. The time when they do that will be a great day for this world—and I firmly believe that, as peoples come to their senses, honest-to-goodness disarmament *will* come. But disarmament can be effective only on a man-to-man, cannon-to-cannon, ship-to-ship basis. Until then we must keep ourselves strong.

I have no basic quarrel with many of the splendid people who are opposing universal military training this time. After the last war I thought as they do now. Today I admire their optimism, hopefulness for a better and a peaceful world. But I cannot forget various phases of World War I and World War II, through which I intimately lived. I believe that perhaps I was closer than most to the thinking in our country as well as to the thinking of European governments. I tried to learn as I went along.

Many of my friends thought I was wrong in 1937 when I warned our country that Hitler was plunging the world into another war. Anyone slightly familiar with the political history of Europe should have seen what was coming.

Our attitude, though well meaning and with the best intentions, is so shaping as again to strengthen Germany. Once more the foolish idea of a strong buffer state! Germany must never be permitted to become strong—no one can foretell to whom she will lend that strength. I do not want to be cruel, but we must be firm. Twice Germany went to war and given the chance she will go to war again. We are making a tragic mistake to play Germany against other European powers. The combination will be quite different the third time. Germany must be occupied until all the children of five years of age today have passed their twenty-fifth birthday, and even after that she must be policed as to armaments.

For all these reasons I see nothing wrong in every youth being given the advantage of training and experience as well as the opportunity of serving his country. The result can be nothing but beneficial to the individual as well as useful to the country.

I hope others will not make an even more tragic mistake than I made in 1919.

4

The problems we faced in Congress in 1919 included, besides fair settlement of war contracts and the establishment of our national defense, help for our soldiers and sailors to get back into civilian life. Congress was prompt and generous to war contractors. It did seem as if the money-makers and profiteers were being better cared for than the men who fought the war.

Soon after the declaration of war, I had introduced a bill in the House providing for reinstatement in government jobs of men who had left them to join the armed forces. It was hard to see how we could expect private citizens to live up to their obligations in rehiring men who had gone to war if the government itself set them a bad example by telling veterans, "no vacancy." But my bill was referred to the Military Affairs Committee and slept there. The Committee on Reform in the Civil Service, of which I was a member during my first term, did nothing about the situation. That committee, as I told the House, was dead. Soon after I got back to the House in 1919, I introduced an amendment to the legislative, executive and judicial appropriation bill providing that all Civil Service employees who had enlisted or been drafted should, upon being honorably discharged from the service, be reinstated in the positions and with the pay they held before they enlisted or were drafted. That amendment was held up on a point of order. Congress seemed in no mood to give soldiers and sailors a square deal.

Early in our post-war session of Congress the problem of Prohibition began to take shape as one of the major difficulties facing this nation. Prohibition had been put over purely as a war conservation measure. The Volstead Act, designed to enforce Prohibition, had not been drawn up by Representative Volstead as chairman of the Judiciary Committee, or any member of that committee. It had been drawn up for them by dry organizations, particularly the Anti-Saloon League. These organizations had no intention of providing real enforcement of Prohibition. If that ever came about, they would have had to go out of business. The only dry organization which I believed to be on the level was the Women's Christian Temperance Union.

In speeches on the floor of the House in favor of Prohibition, a great deal was said about the "foreign element." They were supposed to be doing so much drinking in our large cities. I reminded the House that this so-called "foreign element" was not the consumer of whisky and other hard liquors. They perferred light wines and beer. I also pointed out that most of the foreign-born in our cities had all they could do to buy food and shelter for their families at the high prices prevailing during and especially right after the war. They couldn't afford liquor. Right in my own district, which comprised 250,000 people in the heart of New York City, many of them foreign-born, or the children of foreign-born, you didn't see the excessive drinking.

The House had also been arguing about how much alcohol it took to get a man drunk, and there was a lot of loose talk about the terrible effects of excess drinking. I told the House that I had no knowledge of that because there had been nothing like that in my family or among my associates. "None of my ancestors had that failing," I said. "I traced it way back and the only one of my ancestors I could find who drank to excess was a certain Nero, and he got the habit from his mother who was born on the Rhine."

It seemed to me utterly impossible to establish in an act of Congress how much alcohol should be in a drink. I pointed out that if Congress began that sort of thing, when it came to a tariff act, we would have to determine the difference between a sardine and an anchovy. In July 1919 I predicted to the House:

"I maintain that this law will be almost impossible of enforcement, and if this law fails to be enforced, as it certainly will be as it is drawn, it will create contempt and disregard for law all over this country." The Volstead Act, I maintained, was sure to create drinking of bad liquor throughout the country. We needed education, not prohibition. I also tried unsuccessfully to amend the Volstead Act to provide jury trials to determine all questions of fact instead of permitting, as the act did, injunctions, writs, restraints without trial by jury, granted after someone had taken the word of agents, officers or policemen on questions of fact. Anyone should have been able to see that we were in for a lawless, rowdy era, if we let that vicious act be put on our statute books.

Anti-Semitic riots broke out in Poland soon after the end of World War I. I introduced a resolution instructing our delegates to the Peace Conference "to communicate in clear and non-equivocal language to the representatives of the newly formed governments in whose countries these unfortunate acts have taken place that the United States government and people of the United States cannot understand a people who desire liberty and self-government and will not exercise tolerance in religious worship and restraint and control over unnatural and inhuman hatred, and that the people of the United States can have no friendship for the people of any country who will permit or tolerate such conduct in their country." The resolution also called on our representatives at the Peace Conference to warn such governments that they could expect no assistance from the United States.

This resolution was read at a huge mass meeting in Madison Square Garden. That called attention to the subject throughout the country. The resolution was considered by the House Committee on Foreign Affairs. Within two weeks the State Department issued a statement declaring that satisfactory assurances had been obtained from the Polish government that there would be no repetition of the Jewish pogroms. Some Poles in this country didn't like me after that, and they tried to influence Americans of Polish descent as well as other citizens to vote against me.

Congressmen during my early terms, as well as later, were subjected to many social solicitations, along with the other official and unofficial inhabitants of the nation's capital. In my time as a Congressman there were two well-known lists submitted by professional party planners to aspiring hosts and hostesses. How many such lists there are now I would not know. But everything has expanded greatly since 1919. The names of prospective guests were sold by these social planners at so much per head. Eligible bachelors were particularly desirable. Hostesses picked the ensemble of their dinner, tea and cocktail parties and other functions from these professional lists. A flood of invitations followed, and I got my share. I paid no attention to them.

But I did accept one formal social invitation, aside from

the government functions it was important or useful to attend. I had only recently returned from my war service. Senator William M. Calder, who had represented New York in the House for many years, had befriended me when I first went to Washington. He used to call me "Sonny" and was much concerned for my welfare and future career. Incidentally, though he had so much more experience than I, and disagreed with me on many subjects that came before Congress, he never once attempted to argue with me or put pressure on me about my speeches or my votes.

Senator Calder came to me one day and said that he wanted me particularly to go to a dinner party some friends of his were giving. I told him that I never went to those things. "I know, Sonny," he said, "but this time you've got to do me a favor and come with me." Of course, I accepted the invitation, and to make sure that I got there, Senator Calder called for me at my hotel in his car.

While cocktails were being served, I got into conversation with a gentleman about Croatia and Dalmatia. I didn't like his attitude. "What do you know about Croatia and Dalmatia?" I asked belligerently. "I've lived in that part of the world for three years, and I know what I'm talking about," I told him. "I am the Serbian Ambassador here," my fellow guest replied indignantly.

Then we passed into the dining room. The lady on my left and I got into a conversation about Liberty motors for airplanes. I sounded off and told her how rotten I thought they were, and tore into General Motors in particular. I soon learned that she was related to one of the big shots of that great organization.

After dinner, when I went to the men's room, a man

came in and started a conversation with me. "How do you like the party?" he asked. "Why, I never saw such a bunch of nuts before," I answered. "I'm going. Want to come along?" "I can't," he said, "I'm your host."

I thought my social career was ruined forever, but soon afterwards the same host and hostess wanted to give a dinner party with me as the guest of honor, on the grounds that I had been "so amusing." But not even my good friend Senator Calder could get me to submit to that one. I guess I'm still on the blacklist.

When Congress recessed in the summer of 1919, I planned to put in the time before the next session catching up on reading and studying subjects in which I was particularly interested, such as old age pensions, unemployment insurance and improvements in our labor laws. I had hardly got home to New York, however, when I was informed that the House Military Affairs Committee had resolved to make a tour of inspection in Europe. Since the Republicans had carried the House the previous November, I was placed on that big committee, which was considered a distinct recognition for a young member. Though the new committee had not yet been formally elected by the House, the old committee had extended an invitation to the newly designated members, and I was asked to join the junket.

We left New York on the S.S. *Leviathan*. From the moment I set foot on the ship, until I got back home, I could not help but feel the difference between going overseas as a soldier and going over as a member of an investigating committee of Congress. Take my advice: if at any time you have the choice, pick the latter!

THE END

INDEX